Building Blocks of Innovative Digital Marketing

Building Blocks of Innovative Digital Marketing

Principles that Drive Digital Marketing Success

Bob Shawgo

Topline Frontier

Copyright © 2023 Bob Shawgo. All rights reserved.

Published by Topline Frontier, Eagle Mountain, UT

ISBN: 978-1-962040-00-6

Table of contents

Introduction 1
Intelligence 7
Target 27
Alignment 43
Breadth.. 57
Depth 75
Review 85
Iteration 99
Curation.. 109
References 117

Introduction

As I hurried across the width of campus from my regular class to a lecture I wanted to attend, I kept hoping the opening greetings and introductions would go long. Arthur Henry King, professor emeritus, had come to speak on a topic that was getting a bit of interest around campus. I'd already had to write argumentative papers on the topic in two different classes. It hit at the heart of education and independent thought. The speaker that day needed no introduction. I had heard him talked about throughout my time at the university. Several of my professors had either taken King's classes or been mentored by him. I slipped into the back just as the person conducting finished his introduction of the speaker. Decades have passed since that lecture, but the central message still comes to mind anytime I start to write or present anything instructive. "If education isn't about method, it isn't about anything."

As I've thumbed through the litany of books being churned out on digital marketing. The reason for such a prolific outpouring of content becomes clear. Each book professes to give the reader everything they need to know to get started running digital marketing in their organization. Unfortunately, even though many of the books aren't very old, they might as well be ancient. They list scores of technologies to use and the best ways to use them. The problem with this prescriptive listing of technologies is that most technologies quickly get replaced by newer, better technologies – sometimes multiple times over. A list of specific technologies to use limits both the usefulness of the book and the digital marketer's scope innovation.

My background living through the churn of technologies spans decades. I came into digital marketing when we were building websites page by page in just HTML. JavaScript and CSS were in their infancy and seldom used. Advertising was being bought and sold like magazine ads with pricing based on impressions. Although cookies and sessions existed, little infrastructure existed for digital marketers to take advantage of data. Marketing departments might have a webmaster, who could get some help from designers working across both web and print. In short, everything was pretty static. The closest I came to automating a website on that technology was to create a PERL script that combined an HTML template and a CSV content file to build a few hundred pages for an online catalog. The pages were still manually loaded.

Since that time, I've watched the industry mature and dozens of promising technologies come and go. Along the way, I've tossed out technologies, but hung on to the principles behind their original adoption. The principles were the nuggets of gold plucked from decades of testing, trying, and rebuilding.

I believe the best digital marketing work, the most innovative stuff, is being done by people who push the envelope based on principles. They have a vision of what they want to accomplish and an understanding of the principles at play regardless of technology. They then apply the technology to their advantage.

If you are looking for technical, step-by-step instructions on how to build out a digital marketing machine in your organization, you are looking in the wrong place. You won't find any cookie-cutter approaches about which technologies to link together or how to configure them. You will find principles for building a lasting, evolving digital marketing machine. You'll find time-tested strategies and tactics for managing digital marketing processes, and hopefully, you'll develop a set of habits for evaluating new technologies and approaches in your own digital marketing.

The goal of this book is to give you the foundation to assess circumstances and make decisions about how to build and optimize your digital marketing. Learning about and implementing new technologies is a big part of digital marketing and something you'll do throughout your career. However, the best marketing organizations I've seen aren't the ones jumping onboard with every new plug-and-play technology, but the ones who use technologies according to foundational principles of sound strategy and tactics.

I also wrote this book for marketing leaders who may not be doing hands on production and creative tasks, but need to understand the foundations that go into good digital marketing practices. I recently spent time with a friend in marketing who explained how her company had engaged a firm whose SEO processes were completely outdated. Outdated to the point of having negative consequences on the company's organic search. It became clear that if the leadership in her company were practicing the first three principles of intelligence, target, and alignment, they could have better assessed the agency's proposal and either asked for a revision or gone elsewhere.

Leaders may delegate the investigation of new technologies, but they ultimately have to make decisions. And making those decisions according to time-tested principles greatly improves the odds of choosing wisely.

MARKETING STAGES

For the purposes of analyzing and applying methods to the work we do, marketing is broken out into three distinct stages: Attract prospects, convert leads, and retain customers. Different organizations give different titles to these stages, such as fame, acquisition, and satisfaction. Or they break them into subgroups, like breaking convert leads into nurture and convert. At their core, they are the same three phases. I will refer to these phases and use them to analyze and discuss methodology across the principles that make up the main subject areas of the book.

Attracting prospects is that phase of marketing that we often think of as advertising. It's the delivery of content designed to elicit the first engagement with the customer. These snippets of content are also what well-known brands use to remind would-be customers about their brand.

Converting leads is the work of influencing anyone who has accepted an invitation presented in the attraction phase of marketing. A lead may be known, such as someone who has given you their name and email address, or a lead may be someone unknown who accepted the invitation in your social media ad and clicked through to your website. Anyone who is actively investigating your offering is a lead. This phase of marketing is about influencing them to become a customer.

Retaining customers, though often delegated to departments other than marketing, represents the most stable and cost-efficient revenue generator for the company. Reselling and upselling to current customers should be an essential part of any marketer's strategy, especially digital marketers.

Overlapping principles

The principles in this book should not be thought of as steps. Although I have taken pains to list them in an order that aligns somewhat with where they fall in developing a strategy, they don't have distinct start and end points. Think of them more as considerations. Even as you are gathering intelligence for a new campaign, you are simultaneously considering how to curate the content you already have – filtering out content pieces that don't fit with your updated intelligence.

Each principle acts as a perspective from which to look at your strategy and ensure it is fully formed. And during the execution of your marketing, you can use these same perspectives to shift tactics and improve results. The end goal is that, as a marketer, you are continually thinking in terms of these principles.

From a leadership perspective, leaning more on principles than practices with those you lead can have the effect of generating greater results than prescriptive practices alone would yield. By trusting in the talent of your people to follow the guidance of principles to excel and grow, you allow them to tap into their best work. Rather than thinking of employees as tools that function as an extension of your thinking, focus on sharing the principles and see what kind of bounty you can all harvest together.

CHAPTER ONE

Intelligence

Like any good marketing endeavor – digital marketing starts with intelligence.

> You don't know what you don't know.
> *~ Socrates*

> It isn't what you don't know that hurts you. It's what you know that just ain't so.
> *~ Mark Twain*

I wonder what Mark Twain would think about being quoted next to Socrates. The quote by Socrates is really about broadening an investigation to see more sides of an issue before deciding we know what's going on. The second, by Twain, hints at the hubris that leads us down the wrong road and underscores the need to verify information, especially information we are "sure" about.

Intelligence gathering is both science and art. If you want good actionable data for digital marketing, your gathering needs to be quantitative. And if you want the people consuming the marketing to be engaged and persuaded, your gathering needs to be qualitative. Do you see the difficulty? Information gathering also needs to provide different things at different marketing stages. As I talked about earlier, I'll be looking at this in terms of attracting prospects, converting leads, and retaining customers.

Consider how you go about building a house. When making decisions about a house, you have decisions being made from two directions. You have one group, usually the homeowner, making decisions about the general layout, the colors, surface materials, fixtures, and so on. These are, for the most part, qualitative data points. You also have a second group, generally builders and engineers, making decisions about the size of footings needed, the dimensions and spacing of timber in the floors and walls, the type of roof trusses or rafters, the insulation, the weather proofing for the climate, and so on. These are generally quantitative decisions, driven by the requirements for the house. The decisions made by each group affect the decisions made by the other. These decisions require a lot of back and forth, because it's important that both sides understand each other's decisions. The engineer needs to know that the owner wants a natural stone wrapped fireplace and chimney on the main floor as this changes the structure of the floor and supports below that fireplace.

You face the same thing as a digital marketer. You work with content marketers who gather qualitative information through customer discussions. But their information also needs to be informed by data. The keywords they want to use may not be the keywords people are searching for. By going back and forth between qualitative and quantitative data, you can come to an understanding that will best serve your marketing objectives.

Do I have the marketing intelligence I need to move forward?

At a software company, reports from sales indicated they had all but quit signing prospects up for the company's software trial. This was a free 30-day trial environment that let the prospective client company kick the tires, so to speak. A look at the data showed that the trial was a factor in a dismally low number of sales. Further investigation showed that the reasons behind sales abandonment of the trial included the trial being based in an older version of the user interface. Who wants to recommend a trial that doesn't look like the current production version?

A plan was hatched to, at the very least, shift the trial environment to the latest user interface and create some supporting material that walked the users through key areas of the software. A commitment from sales to use an updated version was tentative. They seemed to take a wait and see approach. Having an up-to-date version seemed to be an imperative regardless of how much use it got. If the trial proved to once again be a factor in sales, part B of the plan was to double down and build out trials that focused on specific industries – such as pointing out warehouse integration for distribution companies and grant tracking for nonprofits.

With a new trial and supporting materials launched, digital marketing began watching the numbers. They stayed low – really low – compared to historical numbers. A deep dive into historical numbers showed a clear drop-off point in trial usage. It didn't coincide with the change in the user interface, which took place over a year after the drop off. Looking at the numbers with a broader team from product marketing revealed that the drop-off coincided with a very successful demonstration campaign that provided a tour of the software in a webinar-style presentation. That had been so successful that industry-specific versions of the tour had also been rolled out, and it was still humming along nicely. Signing up for the demo had essentially replaced signing up for the trial. This intelligence didn't eliminate the need for a trial environment that was up to date – some people would still ask for one – but it did mean putting the brakes on part B of the trial plan.

Assess the information you have now and decide if you have enough to move forward. You will never have all the information, but you have to pull the trigger at some point. Analysis paralysis doesn't put money in the bank. No campaign is perfect, which is why iteration is a key principle of digital marketing. You need a baseline of intelligence to move forward. Deciding what that is early in your project will help you set intelligence milestones toward your launch.

In the example above, the company didn't just steamroll ahead with industry-specific trials based on assumptions. They built in an intelligence milestone between part A and part B of their plan. They also relied on talent from multiple groups to come together in analyzing the issue.

How can I build more intelligence gathering into my digital marketing process?

Allow me to shift gears for a moment to bicycling. When I was considering how to train for my first 200-mile ride from Logan, Utah to Jackson, Wyoming, a friend and veteran rider pointed out that nothing prepared him for the event like participating in the event. He was right. Though I trained hard and did everything I could think of to prepare for that first double century ride, I really had no idea what was needed.

After that first 200-mile ride, I completely changed how I trained for the next year's ride. During that first year I had congratulated myself on little 10-mile Monday morning hill climbs. The next year I would combine multiple mountain and canyon climbs in my Monday morning rides, usually somewhere between 60 and 70 miles, then attack other hills on Wednesday and Friday. Tuesdays and Thursdays were for 20-mile rides to stay fresh. That first year I had started my taper week with a 40-mile ride and dropped mileage each day until the race. The next year and years after, I started my taper week with an 80-mile ride. I also rode differently throughout the summer. Instead of pleasant Saturday morning rides when I was fresh, I practiced standing climbs and long rides at the end of the day when I was already physically and mentally spent from working on my house or doing activities with my family. I did this because I had learned that for most of a 200-mile ride, you feel spent and need mental toughness to keep going. Participating in that first event built intelligence into my training plans that I wouldn't have otherwise had.

As experienced marketers can tell you, more data comes from running a campaign than anything else. Build data collection points into your digital marketing so that the process becomes a feedback loop of intelligence. This can even be a point of competitive advantage as you and your team find innovative ways to glean and use intelligence from your everyday activities. I'll dive into more details about what to collect in the sections devoted to intelligence around attracting, converting, and retaining customers.

What processes do I need to put into place to make sure intelligence is analyzed and acted upon?

One of the most exciting parts of this question to me is its potential for innovation. Note, the question isn't asking what processes you should adopt or asking you to pick from a list of preconceived patterns, but rather it's inviting you to develop processes. And it's asking about processes you need, not your competitors or companies like yours, by you. This is one of those places where good thinking can create competitive advantages.

Intelligence gathering and analysis needs to be part of regular processes, even part of the culture, if it is going to be used effectively. Every campaign, page, and piece of collateral has a data collection component. When the digital marketing team knows where data is being collected and how to pull it together from different sources, they can create more circumspect plans and structures. Because customers are handled by different groups at different points in the lifecycle, data about the customer may end up in different locations. Digital marketing needs the data from every step in the lifecycle to intelligently market to customers during attraction, conversion, and retention.

Digital marketing also needs to follow trends across the lifecycle. Intelligence gathering should be broad enough to understand the full scope of a problem. Like in the above example about the software trial, sometimes having just a part of the picture could lead us down paths where we think we are improving things, but we are really only preparing to waste creative cycles.

When it comes to adding technology to streamline your intelligence processes, consider this word of caution. Add marketing tech after you establish your workflows and best processes. Adding tech before you know what you want often leads to cookie-cutter processes that leave out the most important ingredient – your team's creative genius and innovation. This will always be your biggest competitive advantage. Tech is often built to mimic big company processes or industry standards drawn up by someone else's group think. Group think is beige, and no one notices beige.

Although this chapter is specifically on intelligence, I will continue to refer to intelligence gathering opportunities in later chapters. Now let's look at intelligence as a principle applied in the attract, convert, and retain phases of marketing.

Attract

Attracting customers means giving people the first taste of the brand and the product. Intelligence at this phase of marketing requires answers to certain questions – questions related to immediacy and top-of-mind concerns. It means tapping into the emotions of decision making to capture initial attention.

Why were people attracted to this or similar products?

A maxim as old as marketing is that people first make an emotional connection with a product or service, and only then will they search out information to support their purchasing decision. This means that all attracting starts with making an emotional connection. An emotional connection doesn't need to be overtly emotional. In fact, overtly emotional appeals to the wrong market can turn off prospective customers or come off as unintentionally humorous. The overly emotional ad is a favorite trope of Saturday Night Live satirical ads.

Emotional appeal is often something other than some explicit feature to be explained. Maybe it's the sound of a sports car or steam coming off a freshly baked pizza. Find that emotional hook, and you're on the trail to developing the right messaging, keywords, and so on. This information may come from sales or test marketing of your product, or at early stages, it may come from similar products.

Why did people search or click an ad?

People don't just find you by accident, they searched for something or noticed an ad while viewing related content. What was that? What did a user click on to find you?

It can be a keyword. (Wouldn't that be nice?) It's more likely an idea, a theme, or a style. Consider ways to capture this idea or theme. How do people describe the thing they are looking for? It's rarely just one way, and because it isn't one way, the word cloud becomes your friend. This is a cloud of words and concepts that are larger or smaller, or perhaps positioned more toward the center based on their prominence across searches. Although word clouds had become a fad for a while that seems to have passed, their simplicity as a way to visualize the prominence of concepts is still a strong tool in the digital marketer's arsenal. The advantage over simply making a list is that it shows a relationship based on importance and can be useful for defining clusters or related items that might indicate separate vertical or micro-vertical markets. You can take it a step further and create relationships between words or even relationships between clusters of words.

These words become important because they start to inform your digital campaign with everything from search terms to advertising terms. The best words at this phase of marketing are those words that relate to the emotions of prospects.

What is the emotional appeal? And how aspirational is the emotional appeal? Todd for example, may want a sports car because of what he believes it says to other people about who he is – status. What words do people use when the emotional buy-in is status? They aren't likely to type "social status" because it lacks social cache. Mary, on the other hand, loves the exhilaration she gets when she's behind the wheel on the open road. She might use words related to speed, handling, or performance.

What led people to your content?

This part of your intelligence gathering often reads like a detective story. You look for clues and backtrack the movements of the subject to reveal what led up to the event in question.

If you can back track to the search and the click and the click before that, you are on the trail to find the paths that lead to you. Several technologies do this for you and newer, better technologies show up every year. The key to capitalizing on this intelligence is how you organize it. By organizing it into same, similar, and variant paths you narrow in on points of influence, where you can market. Some roads leading to you are barely travelled and others are highways. Knowing the difference tells you which roads can only be widened a bit and which roads can be turned into superhighways.

What problems do people immediately know they have, that you can solve?

Many of the paths and highways leading to you are aligned with problems people are trying to solve or benefits people want to enjoy. People rarely describe the solution they are looking for in terms of product features. They describe the problem they are trying to solve. Your intelligence should focus on these problems.

People's problems come in a couple of varieties. The most important problems you need to discover and focus on are those that people immediately know they have. If you mention a solution to a problem people don't immediately know they have, you won't capture their attention. Educating people about a problem they don't know they have is a long, uphill (translation: expensive) process.

This is the point where you tell me you have a product that people don't know they need – like the iPhone. They may not know that they want your solution, but they know what they want. Your intelligence needs to dig up the language people would use to describe the readily recognizable benefit they would get from your product.

The key takeaway here is immediate – immediate recognition, immediate comprehension, immediate appeal.

What events may trigger a search for a solution, and can you categorize and track these events in your target market?

This can be a matter of interviewing customers and prospects, as well as a point of data in advanced traffic tracking systems. Building this intelligence into your target profile can be invaluable in finding customers ready to buy. You can also gain intelligence from talking to people within your company who interact with customers, especially of their feedback is evidence based. Avoid making big investments based on phrases like, "I talk to a lot of customers, and I think...." Instead look at what the data shows. If you have people in your organization that talk to a lot of people have them start quantifying their interactions. I attended a customer conference for a software company. Every time I met someone new to the software, I made a point of asking them the same key questions and afterward writing down their answers. Over the three days, I had a piece of marketing intelligence with enough responses to start identifying trends.

Getting in touch with new customers allows you to find answers to questions from their first introduction to your products and brand. New customers have not only the facts of their stories fresh in their minds, but they also have the emotions. Get to the heart of those attraction points and experiences. In his book, *How Customers Think*, Gerald Zaltman deep dives into the interview processes that yield the subconscious motivations that drive customer interest. Through properly worded questions and follow-up questions, you can get to the metaphors that people use to describe their motivating emotions. Across a customer base, similarities start to appear that can form a basis for both search terms and creative messaging.

What kind of media do prospects look for – articles, data sheets, videos, and so on?

In the early days of the internet, media consumption was limited to static webpages. Now, with streaming services and fast downloads, people have no limits to the types of media they can consume about a product. Your intelligence research needs to dig up the types of media your target customers consume. Are they readers looking for deep, insightful articles like professional decision makers? Are they consuming online videos or social media blurbs?

Asking people is a good, direct method, though it should be supplemented with data to refine results. People may be most likely to talk about the validation media they consumed, but to succeed in the attract stage, you want to find what was upstream of that. What created the emotional appeal that led them to consume more media about a product or service? That's the place to focus first.

What social media do they follow?
Reaching teenage boys about your newest video game requires a completely different social strategy than one for reaching the heads of human resource departments about benefits management software. Beyond knowing something about your target customer's preferences, you need to know something about their social channels.

A few months before sitting down to write this book, I came across a book on social media marketing that was mostly lists of social media platforms and technologies to use in attracting customers. The problem with the list was that even though it was only a couple of years old, it was out of date. About half the items on the list were either out of style or had shifted their demographic appeal. Social media is a moving target, which is why current and continuing research is essential.

Often you can determine appropriate social media by demographics and areas of interest. You can narrow down the most popular media for your target audience by tracking where your customers came from. Testing social media channels is worth the effort and the cost. Be warned – you need to do this systematically to avoid excessive spend. Simply throwing content against the wall of social media to see what sticks gives you sporadic results that are hard to replicate. You need to think in terms of systems that allow you to narrow your target and build a strategy.

A strategy I've seen lately – and one that has technology services designed to facilitate it – is to have employees repost company content on their web channels. I have some cautions here for both the employees and for digital marketers. For the employees, if you fill up you social media with promotional materials from your company and nothing else, your followers may begin to tune you out. Share judiciously. You know who follows you. What value does your post bring to them? And for digital marketers, before you start building strategies based on the inflow of clicks from your associates' social media posts, consider carefully, the demographics they represent. The people who follow your CFO are probably (almost certainly) different from the people who follow that nineteen-year-old snowboard freestyler kid from the warehouse. Build social-media intelligence accordingly.

If you do ask employees to repost company posts, be sure that any templates you use are either fool proof or are used by employees with some level of training. I recently ran across a post from a company executive that was obviously from a template. I know this because at the top of the post in brackets were the words "[add your content here]" followed by some boilerplate content from the company. Not an ideal execution.

A downside of this strategy is the difficulty you have in capturing intelligence around such a campaign. You need to build intelligence gathering into your links. You also need know if the link came through your official company channel or somewhere else.

Convert

The intelligence you gathered for the attraction stage of marketing sits upstream from the intelligence you need for your conversion stage strategy. The interested person has moved from being a prospect to being a lead. You may not know his or her name yet, but you should have gathered some intelligence about this person. During the conversion process, you have an emotionally interested lead who wants to validate a purchase. You have two main digital marketing functions during this time: First, feed the lead with the content they want, and second, get out of the way. Every piece of content should invite and entice the customer to learn more.

Your intelligence job as the digital marketer is to discover the line-up of content that most likely leads to conversion. To get started on that, you need to answer some questions. These can be answered directly through interviews or indirectly through following the winding paths of customers through your content. Ideally, you can do both.

Why did people purchase?

Specifically, you want to find out what information about your product led a customer to validate the purchase of your product. It's not just the benefits themselves, but also the value they expect to get from the benefit.

This might be a good time to mention that customers come with different talents for extrapolation. To be able to extrapolate is what I like to call vision. Some customers exhibit more vision then others. They can see the potential for a product or service in their life and make the leap to come up with the value all on their own. Other customers need hints to lead them to the value. If you can understand the value customers get from your product, you can find ways to clarify and simplify the content to express that value. It's the difference between saying, "Hotel members get late checkout." vs. "Hotel members can sleep in, thanks to late checkout." Later checkout is a benefit; sleeping in is value.

Why now?

Find out what events led them to spend time looking into your product. These events may lead you to understand the value that people are looking for. Don't be contented with the short answer. Deeper questions and answers lead you to deeper understanding of the larger categorization of events that lead to customer conversion. For instance, a customer may tell you that your product looked like it would lead to greater employee satisfaction. A little digging may reveal that employee attrition over reporting regulations had led to a downturn in sales and customer satisfaction. The customer has given you a nugget of intelligence to use with customers in similar circumstances.

Why now might also have to do with market conditions. You may find that sales made in a strong economy won't be made in a weak economy or vice versa. You might also uncover purchasing cycles. Almost every business has an annual cycle. Knowing that annual cycle can help you understand when to press for conversion and when to wait. A housewares, small appliance company I worked with, found over several years that channel buying by stores was cyclical on an annual basis and that sell through to customers aligned with the economy. The first point determined when stores would buy, and the second how much they would buy. In a down economy, customers were more likely to buy small items like new blenders and toasters in place of larger purchases like furniture and cars.

How did they decide among products?

What did customers see in your product that they didn't see in a competitor's product? This is the kind of intelligence that can make or break your conversion offerings and content efforts. When asked why they purchased a product, people tend to answer with features. Just listing features doesn't help you reinforce the emotional bond your customer developed with the product and brand. You need to dig deeper than the feature answers. You need to find out what value the product created in the customer's life that they didn't expect to get from other products.

What about the product and the purchasing process was most important to them?

When the customer started looking into the product, certain aspects of the product or the company or the buying process stood out as most important to them. Hierarchies exist in almost everything we do, and this includes in how we choose the products and services we purchase. Map those hierarchies so you can create an optimal flow. Which of those three – product, company, and buying process – mattered most and how did it create value? Perhaps your business relies on aspects of the offering other than those three. Whatever they are, discover the hierarchy among them. Then you can focus on the area most likely to convert a lead to a customer.

Don't underestimate ease of purchase as a selling factor. Every time I log into Amazon, it shows me a little display of frequently or recently purchased items. That little feature ensures I change the water filter in my fridge because it's easy. Many of the things people buy are bought because they were easy to obtain.

Consider the ease with which the lead accesses product and company information. Is gating content helping or hurting your process? More than once I've started to sign up for a piece of content or a webinar only to cancel the process because the vendor required too much information. Making access fast, easy, and painless may have more to do with conversion than grabbing as much information as possible on the first contact.

Gathering information directly

The two-edged sword of gated content is this: You can gather intelligence about a lead, or you can turn away a potential lead by over asking. Even interested people drop off when you start asking too many questions early in the conversion process. As a general rule, I like to gather direct information a little bit at a time. When asking for a piece of information like a phone number or email address, it's important to have a compelling reason that benefits the prospect. Go ahead and be overt about telling them the reason. Also, and this might be a personal pet peeve, if you ask them the name of the company they work for, unless you're dealing with a high-volume sign-up event, don't then ask for a bunch of information about the company like headcount and annual revenue. Carry your own water. You can look that stuff up. If you can't find that information, the company is likely a small business, and you can act accordingly.

Retain

Only focus on gathering intelligence for customer retention if you want to increase profit margins. Your existing customers are your most profitable because the cost of influencing repeat purchases, upgrades, and upsells are considerably lower than with new customers. If your business legitimately doesn't have repeat customers, then skip this section.

Retaining customers may seem to be out of the scope of digital marketing intelligence. This is why so few companies create workable strategies around customer retention. They lack both the data gathering and the digital strategy to systematically retain customers. They also lack the intelligence gathering to determine what upgrades will most delight current customers.

The best source of intelligence is your own customer base. Your next best source is your employees who interact with customers. These discussions can be tricky, as people often tell you what they think you want to hear. This is why a few anecdotes may get you started but will never make for a lasting, data-centered strategy.

A lasting strategy means continuously gathering reviewing and updating the answers to customer retention questions.

Why have people stayed with this or similar products?

The reasons satisfied customers stay with your product gives you intelligence in the key factors to build on in your customer retention campaigns and content. Following up on this question and getting detailed answers helps you gather specific problems solved and emotional connections customers may have to your product and brand.

Why purchase again?
Customers who make repeat purchases can provide direct information on what can lead other customers to do the same thing. Like converting leads, pay special attention to what events lead up to repeat purchases. Also pay attention to language about the customers attitude toward the product and the repeat purchasing process.

Why upgrade?
Similar to purchasing again, upgrading indicates a deeper commitment to the product and brand. As with a repeat purchase, pay close attention to events in the customer's life or in their company that may have prompted the upgrade.

How do they make the decision on whether to stay?
Understanding the decision process, including who is involved and the timing of such decisions, helps you see where you can strengthen your customer retention campaigns by broadening your audience, by adjusting your timing, or by some other factor brought to light by the customer.

What criteria are involved in continuing with the product?
Customers, especially business customers, may have lists of criteria that must be maintained for them to stay with the product. Knowing what these are, and the hierarchy of the checklist, can give you clues into what is vital to customers. It can help you craft campaigns that help remind other customers why customers choose and stay with your product or brand.

The focus of your interviews
When interviewing customers, you need to focus as much on the words they choose to use as on the ideas they express. Most people want to be seen as making decisions based on rational reasons. Customers at-

tempt to convey reasons that are rational. The language and metaphors they use can point you to the emotional connections they have with the product or service. They also point you to the aspects of the product value that matter most to customers.

Delight your customers

What customer interviews won't point you to directly is what you need to do next to delight your existing customers. Your customers can easily tell you what they want, and when you give it to them, you've done what they expected, not what will delight them. When you give them what they asked for, the response is somewhere between, "Thank you" and "Well, it's about time." If you want to delight your customers, you need to give them what they weren't expecting. That comes out of the language your customers use.

You might think that delighting customers with product advancements is out of scope for digital marketing. But how can the company best reach customers to shout about their new products without engaging digital marketing. The greatest digital campaigns you run among your current customers will be those that tap into what delights them – where they have an emotional connection. As a digital marketer, you are the keeper of intelligence on this front. You keep track of the campaigns that get great response and those that are ho-hum. Your analysis is vital to producing more of the former and less of the latter.

Summary

Keep two things in mind when gathering intelligence: first, do enough research to know what you don't know, meaning find out the areas where you lack data, and second, challenge the assumptions you have going in to be sure that they are correct.

Find answers to the following:

- Do I have the marketing intelligence I need to move forward?

- How can I build more intelligence gathering into my digital marketing process?
- What processes do I need to put into place to make sure intelligence is analyzed and acted upon?

For attracting prospects:
- Why were people attracted to this or similar products?
- Why did people search or click an ad?
- What led people to your content?
- What problems do people immediately know they have, that you can solve?
- What events may trigger a search for a solution, and can you categorize and track these events in your target market?
- What kind of media do prospects look for – articles, data sheets, videos, and so on?
- What social media do prospects follow?

For converting leads:
- Why did people purchase?
- Why now?
- How did they decide among products?
- What about the product and the purchasing process was most important to them?

For retaining customers:
- Why have people stayed with this or similar products?
- Why purchase again?
- Why upgrade?
- How do they make the decision on whether to stay?
- What criteria is involved in continuing with the product?

CHAPTER TWO

Target

"Who's your target market?" the marketing consultant asks.

The most common client answer is "Everybody!" The client, somehow knowing this is the wrong answer, begins laying out evidence of why everybody is going to want their product.

The next question is a simple way to create a reality check. "How much money do you have to market to everybody?" In other words, let's figure out who wants your product the most and figure out what segment of that group we can afford to market to.

Essentially, your target is a function of those ready to buy over marketing dollars to spend. With this in mind, much of creating a target is cutting a total addressable market down to size. If you aren't willing to cut your market down to size, you will burn through your budget with all the inefficiency of a dot com company buying a Super Bowl ad in 2000. Getting to a finely tuned target is about getting your maximum return on investment. Make sure every marketing dollar you cast upon the water comes back buttered.

Keeping the target principle in mind helps you build a focused and efficient digital marketing strategy. That strategy is about more than just the target market. I've seen companies tightly define a target market in media and advertising buying only to push out generic messaging written for their "everybody" audience. Whenever the principle of target comes up, discussion initially goes to target market, and that's a big part of it. As you'll see, another vital part of target is how well you have targeted or focused your offer. Does the language and the imagery of your campaigns and content focus on your target market's interests? How might that interest level be raised by further focusing your target? Are you using the language that your target buyer uses? For instance, if you are marketing your service to not-for-profits, you refer to the customer organization, not the business. You talk about the mission and stewardship, not profit and ROI.

If you think your organization has one grand message that resonates across all demographics, regions, and industries, you need to go back to the first principle and gather more intelligence.

The wrong market underperforms

It's not that your offering isn't any good, it's that you pointed it at people who just weren't the most interested. Sometimes people start companies with hunches of who their target market is. If they are smart, they make low cost, low fidelity pitches to members of this target market. This may simply be a marketer with a PowerPoint and a brief demo. What is being gauged here is interest?

If the response is positive, it is followed with some low spend digital marketing. Does the target respond? Does the response warrant further spend or further testing?

If the response is negative, you just haven't identified those most likely to buy. Talk to more people. One technique that can be used during startup or when considering expansion into a new industry is to attend events and just talk to people. A sports biotech company I worked with used this method. We identified potential markets and signed up to have a booth at events tailored to those markets. I know this isn't exactly digital marketing, but conversations with people at those events generated messaging and points of interest for our digital campaigns. The events were fairly inexpensive, while the human interaction about the brand was priceless.

The issue may come back to what I mentioned earlier. A target market that's too broad can be just as ineffective as a disinterested target. Though it may seem that you're making sales, they are coming at too high a cost.

You may think that targeting a broad market will give you the intelligence to narrow your market based on who is most likely to buy. The problem is that a broad market means you're employing messaging that is so vague, it doesn't appeal to anybody. You're spending a lot to put a message in front of people that just doesn't speak to them.

Target efficiency

I sat in a meeting with a head of marketing who quipped, "We can't afford to buy TV advertising across the whole country, we'll probably just start with New York and California."

Based on what? Is it because they are big markets? Forget about the fact that you don't buy advertising by state, you should know the efficiency of your targets before you spend a dime on them.

Let me give you a digital marketing example. When working on marketing a software product for small to medium businesses (SMB) where our target audience was the CFO, we set about to improve the upper end, the medium-sized part, of our business. After a bit of intelligence gathering, we determined that the main difference between sales engagements in small businesses vs. medium-sized businesses was the inclusion of the IT department in the decision making. We pursued the idea of marketing to IT professionals in the SMB space. After developing a skeleton of a plan, we determined that marketing to IT for our software was too expensive. Because IT worked on software across an organization, any marketing of finance-specific software targeting IT would require such a high frequency to cut through the noise of other marketing that it would cost more than it was worth. We settled on a plan to educate the CFO on mid-market IT concerns during the conversion phase of marketing, so the CFO could be our champion when IT joined the approval process.

Unit cost, a big part of honing a digital advertising strategy, like a traditional advertising campaign, comes down to efficiency. Let me restate a question raised earlier. Are you reaching the most people ready and willing to buy with the money you're spending? In traditional broadcast advertising, you set a budget, set a target market, set a frequency, and then buy as efficiently as you can to get the greatest lift in sales. Efficiency doesn't mean you buy the cheapest markets; it means you buy the markets that make the most efficient use of your money while giving you the greatest return.

The way to do this without bias toward hunches is to create a market index based on factors that influence sales. In digital marketing, your target market tends to have an affinity for certain keywords and media types. Your keyword and media efficiency index will likely be a factor in creating your overall efficiency index. Another factor may be category awareness and brand awareness among a given target. Consider these factors against the cost of hitting your frequency goals for a target, and you can create an index to guide you in buying efficiently.

Addressable target

Targets are about more than identifying potential customers. They are also about identifying addressability of your market. The classic story of a startup going into their first pitch with investors claiming to have a vast addressable market, presupposes they have the means or will get the means to get in front of that market. Your digital addressable market may only be a portion of your total market. Even now, with constant access, digital marketing channels still don't reach everyone. You need to come up with a truly addressable target market. We've heard a lot about how digital marketing became a factor in political campaigns over the past several US national elections. Yet for the portion of the electorate that votes in the highest percentage, senior citizens, outreach still needs to be by mail or in person.

Also, for services, you may be limited by geography. For expensive products you might be limited by affordability. As you move from attract into convert and then to retain, the focus narrows and splits.

You also need to consider your target market's access. You not only want to narrow your market focus; you want to also identify the channels and media types most consumed by your target market. In short, can you provide content to the target market? For example, elderly men who hate the internet are not a target market for digital marketing. Move on. Also, people who do all their browsing on their phones may require a different media approach than a professional buyer working on a computer – especially if you're relying on demos of desktop software.

Converting your focus areas to actionable data for digital marketing may seem at times subjective, but tight, well-constructed targets create patterns for replication as your business grows.

Attract

The digital marketer, as well as the whole marketing team, absolutely must gain a clear sense of their target.

You have several tools at your disposal during the attraction phase to hone your target.

- Borrow
- Observe
- Test
- Interview

But wait, you're saying, "Isn't that intelligence gathering?" To which I say, "Yes, yes it is." The principles of digital marketing are full of overlap. They are related and intermingled. That's why they are all part of one core business function.

Borrow

What if, like every startup everywhere, you don't yet have any customers? And of course, you've already realized you won't make the classic blunder of thinking everyone is your customer. You just haven't yet identified the customer you ought to target. Luckily for new companies or new products, you aren't the first or likely the only one selling in your category.

Borrowing is the strategy of finding the target market of a similar sales channel or product and using it as a surrogate until you can hone your own unique target market.

Have you ever hung out with snow boarders? Living in Utah for a few decades, I've had the chance to hang out with some pioneers of the sport. I'm not talking about any of the legends that turned it into an industry. I'm talking about the teenagers who screwed straps to boards, tied them to their feet, and plunged down mountains in the backcountry. This was before any ski resorts allowed snowboarding. This was at the infancy of the sport. If I were starting the first snowboard company today, I would look at those teenagers and ask myself, "Who do they remind me of?" Then I would remember my own teenage years in Southern California skateboarding in empty pools and on any interesting slab of concrete that didn't have a "no skateboarding" sign. I would borrow from the skateboard industry to figure out how to reach that most-likely-to-buy snowboarder market. Obviously, that market has since matured and split into mature segments, but startup principles are still the same.

Do you want a more current example? Let's say Target, the big box store, decides to pick up your product and is doing fairly well with it. You could decide to focus your digital marketing on the same market that Target stores focus on. Though they carry lots of products, you will find that they have a clear sense of their primary buyers in terms of demographics. This can give you a place to start your digital marketing.

Observation

Observe current sales. Who is deciding to buy? What do they have in common with others deciding to buy?

We tend to think in terms of buyers being in a particular business function, like the example earlier of the CFO or IT professional. Or for consumer goods, we look at a demographic like middle income women between 30 and 50. Don't limit yourself to obvious categories like occupation or demographic. Look at other factors like hobbies, geography, work schedule, etc. Your goal isn't to create an overly cumbersome target profile, rather it is to identify trends that you can capitalize on to reach people who are most likely to buy.

Perhaps you're able to observe, and gather data on, events happening that lead people to use your product or service. Maybe you find a trend among customers that they are most likely to buy when their employee count goes over 100. Maybe your product is perceived as a gift, and you can tie it to people searching for wedding gifts or something kids need when they're starting college. Whatever the event, if it shows a trend, you can track activity related to that event and make sure your offering is a part of it.

I would caution you about trying to tie yourself to huge events, like a pandemic. Unless you are a huge brand, you probably don't have the budget to break through the noise of everyone else trying to tie themselves to the huge event. This doesn't mean you should ignore it, you still want to remain relevant. When the COVID pandemic started, a company I was working with realized that their messaging referred to high-growth companies. With businesses barely hanging on, that messaging suddenly sounded out-of-touch. They quickly shifted messaging to make it more relevant to the situation many businesses found themselves in.

Continued observation will inform you not only about the messaging to be delivered in your marketing, but also how you can best align with search results around key topics.

Testing

No data-centric plan is complete without testing. Testing your way to the right target market takes both patience and some clever, disciplined planning. Typical testing, like A/B testing ad copy, gives clear results based on simple response rates. Testing your way to a target market can require knowing more about people browsing your site or hitting a landing page.

You can test for everything from words used in an ad to images used on a web page. Although you'll run into descriptions of lots of testing like A/B testing, multi-variant testing, and incremental testing, they all eventually narrow down to A/B testing – comparing one option to another. Without getting into too much philosophy, our logic system is still true and false logic. Multi-variant testing tests multiple factors at the same time but will be run repeatedly until it comes down to a binary choice. Incremental testing – where you see the results of adding a new element vs. not adding – is an A/B test as well. Keep that in mind as you try to test complex campaigns and webpages.

Testing can quickly lead you down a rabbit hole of analysis for analysis sake if you don't keep in mind the purpose of the test. You want lots of data points helping you learn something about your target prospect.

Gathering where prospects clicked before they reached you or what version of a campaign they may have responded to is the first step. You may even choose to subscribe to services that build data profiles of prospects to help you identify visitors with the markers that indicate how likely they are to buy. Continuing to gather intelligence on return visitors helps build an interest profile that will help you structure the strategy for your next stage of marketing.

Interviewing

Before I jump into interviewing as a method for defining a target market in the attraction phase, let me shine some light on the interview process. First, an interview is not a survey. You aren't trying to find out which toothpaste four out five dentists recommend. You are trying to get at what factors lead the person to respond to an advertisement. You are trying to understand the viewpoint of the person you are interviewing. And more deeply than that, you are trying to get at the metaphors they use to talk about their interaction with your marketing, the product, and the brand. Metaphors rise out of their subconscious, emotional connections. This means you need to ask questions and follow-up questions. You don't settle for yes or no or simple comparison answers. When someone says things got better, you ask, "In what way?" and "How much better?" When someone says things changed, you ask them to describe how things changed and what the impact was on the people in the company.

Specific to the attraction stage of marketing, your interview needs to focus on things that will inform your ability to attract additional prospects. What was going on in their life or their business? What problem were they experiencing or what aspiration did they hope to fulfill? Just like in your intelligence gathering, you want to listen not just to the thing they are telling you, but to the words they are using to tell it to you. Words convey emotion. What is the emotional weight of the words they are choosing to use? Were they pleased to solve a problem or were they on the verge of dying if they didn't find relief? If they say the service was "a life saver," they've given you a powerful metaphor. They've let you know that to them the stakes were as serious as life and death. Dig deeper. Did they mean they saved the life of the company, or did they mean they got their life back by no longer spending nights and weekends putting out fires? "Putting out fires" is another strong metaphor. Dig in and see what it means to them.

The attraction phase is all about emotional connection, so the strength and immediacy of an emotional connection will help you find your target market. A broad range of people may have clicked through on your ad for a variety of reasons. Your interviews will reveal which ones had the greatest emotional connection with your ad. This group is the one you should focus on. Now you need to find out things about that group that are actionable in your digital marketing strategy – things like keywords, content consumption, browsing habits, etc.

Convert

Where attraction is often like a funnel, starting broad and narrowing, the conversion phase needs to be even more tightly honed to the target. During the conversion phase prospects are actively investigating your product. They will be consuming detailed information fit to their situation. From a digital marketing standpoint, they need a targeted path to follow that leads them from broad content that helps them know what they don't know to details of the things they've learned about and want to dig deeper into. Creating structures that allow leads to self-select a conversion pathway and then tracking that path will help you serve the targets that are most likely to buy. You might think of this as a purchase on Amazon, where you can offer up content based on previously consumed content. This is what streaming channels call "Viewers who watched A were also interested in B." You might start out by offering up multiple items, and then as patterns emerge, start narrowing the options to the ones most likely to lead to conversion.

Targeting during the conversion phase is also where you have opportunities to identify adjacent markets. As prospects become more involved in researching your product, they are more apt to share information about themselves. This information helps you see trends among users that may help you identify more users. If you discover that 21% of your prospects bought a new home in the last year, you may be able to use that to break them out as a segment to expand on.

Let me also issue a caution on splitting out adjacent markets. The sort of collateral presented at this phase of marketing is often longer and more expensive to create and maintain than what you created for the attraction phase. This means that you don't want to waste content development cycles aimed at weak or limited targets.

We can look at the same target definition methods for the convert stage – borrow, observe, test, and interview – as we did in the attract stage, but with some variations.

Borrow

At this point, you're going to borrow methodology. How are adjacent, successful companies deploying their conversion phase collateral? Notice that I said adjacent, successful companies, not competitors. Let's face it, if you are doing the exact same thing as a competitor, you aren't using your competitive advantage – whatever it is (by this point, know your competitive advantage). When choosing these adjacent companies, consider their place in the company growth cycle, because what a new company deploys to convert innovators and early adopters is not the same as what a more established company deploys to convert early majority customers (see Geoffrey Moore's *Crossing the Chasm*).

Observe

Observation of digital interactions at this phase focuses on what gets used and what is seldom opened. The lead, who you have some data on at this point, will show you their path through content. This is where you can learn video length preferences, follow-up email open rate, and other data points that help you identify patterns and trends in your leads' activities and tighten the path that guides them from attraction to purchase. What kept them engaged? And where did they drop off? And most importantly, what did the ones who bought have in common? What about their behavior identifies them as a target?

A big area to observe to establish your target at this point is the amount of effort that goes into justifying the buying decision. You will have some outliers who analyze to death, but among your purchasers, what amount of content did they regularly consume in their conversion phase. You can start rating these and compare them with those who did not buy or even those who took a long time to buy. Remember that story I related about updating the software trial. That project started with looking at factors of engagement that led to conversion.

Test
You have so many things to test and so little time in the conversion phase. Remember, even if you start with multi-variant testing, you'll eventually need to boil it down to some actionable A/B decisions. Discovering your prime target through testing requires that you know something about them, and you gather data that can lead to a clearer sense of your target. Given options that relate to their identity, what content do they choose? You could present choices of content based on company size, preferred activities, or some other aspect of the customer that helps you identify them. For example, a bicycle company might offer content around road and mountain biking, touring and racing, or human powered and electric. Tracking content choices along with who ultimately purchases increases your awareness of the target customer.

Interview
Interviewing customers about how well conversion materials answered their questions and what might have been lacking can reveal a lot about who among your leads are most likely to go on to become customers.

The interview also gives you an open forum to understand those quantifiable factors that led them to engage with some materials over others. This can cover both the content itself and the media used to deliver it. You can start to see target customers in clusters and understand which ones you need to focus on to get the most profitable sales.

Retain

To be honest, when I first considered the target principle in terms of retaining customers, I had trouble seeing how it applied. Then I started to think about things like net promoter score and customers who evangelize the business and realized that even though we want to retain all our profitable customers, we do have decisions to be made about spending money on marketing campaigns to existing customers. Let's walk through some of the types of customers we want to focus on. Be aware also, that a customer may land in more than one of these categories.

Evangelists

An evangelist customer is gold. What can you do as a digital marketer to identify evangelist and potential evangelist customers? How about looking for trends in content consumption? You can track responses to calls for feedback – like invitations to be on a customer response committee or to speak at a customer conference. You can run customer surveys and look for indicators of high satisfaction. You can interview evangelists and find out what makes them so excited about sharing the product.

An evangelist is more than just a satisfied customer who has good, "quotable" results for a case study. An evangelist creates buzz in the industry and actively promotes your product to their friends. They aren't professional influencers looking for a payday from talking up your products. They are visionaries who are sold on the value they derive and the potential they see in your product.

Most profitable

Not everyone has the personality or inclination to be an evangelist, but that doesn't mean they aren't highly profitable customers. The steady, pay-on-time, repeat-buying customer is the foundation of a profitable business. Working with finance to establish a profile of a profitable customer can help you decide where to spend those customer retention campaign dollars.

On the flip side, depending on your business, you might also get finance to help you identify unprofitable customers. I'm not suggesting a campaign inviting them to move on to other services – though that might be money well spent. Rather, you can cull certain profiles from campaigns, so you aren't spending inefficiently.

Most likely to upgrade

Years ago, I reviewed the marketing processes of a large real estate agency. Whenever they listed a house, they would create a postcard about it and send that card to everyone within a couple of miles of the listing address. They had determined that the most likely buyer of a home was someone who already lived in that area – someone who might want to upgrade or downsize but didn't want to change the stores they shopped at or the schools their kids went to.

Similarly, most businesses have those customers who are more likely than others to upgrade to new products or buy add-ons to products. These are the customers worth the spend of going above and beyond to make sure they know what's available. Maybe you let them know or create offers for them based on their history of growing with the business. The way to find these people is to actively collect and review sales data.

In a retail business, you might find them by establishing an activity basis. Back to our biking example, a recreational bicyclist may be less likely to upgrade than a competitive cyclist, so you could tie your upgrade marketing efforts to competitive events. Learn the activity-based indicators for your business and find ways to reach your most likely target customer.

Summary

Your target is a function of those ready to buy over marketing dollars to spend. Build a focused and efficient digital marketing strategy by always keeping the *target* principle in mind. Don't expect to find one grand message that resonates across all demographics.

Two of the most often overlooked factors in defining your target market that later fall to digital marketing are efficiency and addressability. Efficiency is about reaching and converting as many customers as possible while maintaining a healthy profit, while addressability covers your actual ability to reach prospective customers.

Four ways to define your attraction and conversion target markets are:
- Borrow
- Observe
- Test
- Interview

To build your business among customers, focus on three key types of customers:
- Evangelists
- Most profitable
- Most likely to upgrade

CHAPTER THREE

Alignment

Hopefully, as you begin to gather intelligence, and settle on a target market, you have a sense of what you need to do to align your offering with customer expectations – what we'll call product and message alignment. The alignment I'm referring to in the alignment principle is something different. I'm referring to alignment across your digital marketing offering, right down to internal alignment on each webpage you post.

Imagine you start reading a book about a boy who is supposed to go to the village and sell the family cow. Have you heard this one? On the way, he meets a spy named Bond, James Bond, and the spy needs his help to… wait, that's not how I expected it to go. The story becomes confusing. The whole framing of the story and where it goes is off. This isn't the twist of a good story, it's incongruous. The lack of internal alignment goes against our expectations so strongly that the whole thing turns to a farce. A poorly executed digital marketing framework is similar. If a campaign and content don't align across the various parts then the whole thing loses its veracity both to search engines and to people.

Consider a well-honed, masterfully intelligent search engine reading your web page. It doesn't start with the words on the page. It starts with the meta-data, like the title and meta-description. It then moves on to the top heading on the page – the human readable H1 title – to see what the page is about. It then reads the content of the page to see if the page talks about what the title, the meta-description, and the H1 heading said the page would be about. Because it reads a lot, the search engine is very intelligent. It can tell if a page is providing valuable content for people or if it's just trying to trick the search engine into giving it an unwarranted higher ranking.

In this chapter, we'll first look at this internal alignment needed for organic search. We'll also look at content alignment needed for attracting, converting, and retaining customers. You need to think about how each step in a prospect, lead, or customer journey links to the one before it and the one after it. You also need to consider how alignment is facilitating or disrupting conversion at each stage.

ALIGN WITH ABSOLUTE CLARITY ABOUT WHO YOU ARE ALIGNING FOR

Humorist Dave Berry wrote, "Someone who is nice to you, but rude to the waiter is not a nice person." In the same vein, content that appeals to company executives but not customers is not good creative. When you have content that doesn't appeal to customers, you are failing at the prime purpose of marketing – to create a customer. When you have content that company executives dislike – in the majority, not just that one odd-ball finance guy (yes Ted, I mean you) – it's because the content somehow violates the stories that executives are telling themselves about the company. What are those stories? How do you address them and also get to creative content that moves the needle with customers?

Start by understanding the customer and ensuring that first and foremost the content influences *them*. Content that appeals to executives without influencing customers is just vanity. Vanity projects have no place in marketing that seeks to efficiently influence people to make the journey from prospect to customer.

However, you also need internal alignment, because you need people within the company to rally behind the content you present. I've found that success has a huge rallying effect. But if an ad campaign is effective yet somehow embarrassing to executives, especially sales executives, then you have a problem. They will tell their own stories that contradict the story you are telling. This is an indication of not just a content problem, but a culture problem.

As a digital marketer, you might be saying to yourself, "This is a content problem, not my problem." But I guarantee that misaligned content is everybody's problem. When marketing doesn't make its numbers, it will be all hands on deck – digital and content creators alike. In my experience, it is digital marketing – the results reporters – that call everyone to the table for campaign analysis.

Alignment across stages

Remember when we talked about how people emotionally connect first and later do the research to support their decision to others? This comes up in alignment in a big way. As prospects become leads who become customers, they will need to be reminded of the emotional connection that initially caught their attention. Even as they deep dive into the value proposition of the offering, they will need reassurances that they will get the emotional fulfillment that first attracted them to the product or service. As the keeper of the pathway, the digital marketer can create this alignment across content presented to the customer.

For example, let's assume your customer sees an ad that says, "Make money in your sleep with the Cloud Widget Investment Dohicky." The prospect clicks to learn more, and they end up on a landing page about how the Cloud Widget Investment Dohicky company is ending hunger in central Africa. That's a great endeavor and may be useful information to share at some point, but it doesn't reinforce the prospect's demonstrated interest in making money in their sleep.

This may be an overly simplified example, but how about an ad that says, "Cut your sales cycle in half" that leads to a page with a headline "Number One in CRM Customer Satisfaction." The customer now has to dig to find out about that "cutting the sales cycle" business the ad mentioned. It might be easier to just click back to where they were before and keep scrolling.

Alignment is about creating consistent pathways that build on topics in which the customer has already shown interest.

Alignment across webpages

A big part of alignment is going to deal with web pages. One element often at the hub of digital marketing is the web site. I think this is a good time to discuss differences among the web pages we'll be referencing. Webpages come in different flavors. Two pages are used more than any other and are of special interest to digital marketers. You have pages on your website that can be found using the navigation – core website pages. You also have pages often called landing pages that are built outside of your website navigation. These relate to specific email, digital advertising, or other campaigns – any campaign that needs to link back to a specific topic.

You have additional pages to assist the customer such as resource pages and FAQ pages. You also have pages that structurally flesh out the modern website such as about, contact, privacy, and so on. We will deal less with these and more with the first two.

Attract

In the attraction phase, alignment can make or break organic search.

A few months ago, I was driving through Evanston, Wyoming and wanted to stop for burgers at Wendy's. I had been there before but couldn't remember which freeway exit to take. In a responsible hands-free fashion, I asked my phone to find Wendy's restaurant. It seemed confused, so asked for the "address" to Wendy's restaurant. It shared the address of my neighbors, Steve and Wendy. Not helpful. To the point, search lacking context is not always what we expect, and sometimes you're on your own to find a burger.

Alignment in organic search

What if every search was personally managed by an actual person? What if that person read your search request and understood the context of the search – like a thoughtful person might? What if every query was answered like a knowledgeable friend might answer your question? This is where search is going, and each day it's inching closer to achieving that goal. In fact, with the eventual perfection of chat AI, search should become very much like talking to a friend.

As organic search improves, it not only understands queries more like a person would, it judges web content more like a person would. If you have never read old "web-optimized" copy stuffed with keywords regardless of their impact on content readability, then you are lucky. Even the creators of the content knew that it was so bad that they would create multiple versions of the copy and hide the stuff they only wanted the search engine to see.

On the subject of keywords, let me emphasize that the importance of keywords has not diminished. Words matter because they are the tool we use to communicate ideas. And as much as art and design are a big part of creating an emotional connection with people, words are the clearest medium currently understood by both people and computers. Keyword choice and inclusion is essential to making your content work. And the right keywords help you get found.

Let me share an example. I worked on messaging for a financial management system. And that's the phrase we used, "financial management system." At the company's price point, that term inferred more value than the term "accounting system," which tended to be used for lower-cost systems. As our SEO team dove into keyword impact on search engine optimization, they found that people looking for a product in that category weren't searching "financial management" but instead typed "accounting" into the search bar. We adjusted.

In some cases, search engines will infer additional search terms. Like "bike" for "bicycle." But the challenge of the marketer is still to make sure they have alignment on the keywords that get results. Obviously, not every important keyword can be part of your title or your heading. This is why you have to settle on the most important keyword and rank others below that. And since you want your content to appeal to people, you have to be willing to leave less important keywords out.

I can't over stress the power of a well-formed page where the title, meta-content, H1 headings, and body all align. What exactly does that look like?

I have a title that tells exactly what the page is about. It has one or two of my keywords. This is the title that shows up in the search engine and in the browser title bar, so it needs be readable by people and it needs to attract interested prospects. This is the title of your book or the leading hook article on the front of a magazine. It's also a promise to what the page is about.

Next I have a description, also called a meta-description, that tells more descriptively what the page is about. It contains your top keywords, so that it can assist the search engine. It is also what shows up in search under your page title. So, like the title, it needs to be readable and attractive to prospects.

You can also set meta-keywords and other meta-data that doesn't get displayed to the user, but this seems to be of little concern to search engines.

Next we come to the body of the page – the stage where your content goes on display for the viewer. The main H1 heading is essentially the title of the page for viewers. To maintain logical flow for people and search engines, this should align and perhaps even repeat the page title you placed in the head of the page. A title here that doesn't align with the title the viewer clicked on in the search engine or in an ad creates confusion and possibly disrupts the customer journey.

Next comes the content of the page. Ask a dozen SEO experts about the proper mix of keywords in the body copy of a page, and you'll likely get a dozen different answers. Each has their own secret sauce to sell you that don't really amount to significant differences in outcome. The consensus among people who build lots of sites and who have tested and hacked their way through SEO since the 1990s tends to be this: write your content to be read by people and be sure to include your keywords where they make sense. My three rules for writing successful body copy are simple:

1. Write for people
2. Include keywords
3. Stay on topic

I hadn't really touched on that last one until now, but the real point is about simplicity. Think of a search engine as a young person with an attention disorder. If you go too far afield from the topic at hand, the search engine will get distracted by your additional topics. Or it could downgrade you for not talking about what you said you were going to talk about. This doesn't mean you can't use similes, metaphors, or analogies, after all, our first rule is to write for people. Writing something like, "Our shoe covers are like umbrella's for your feet," won't make a search engine suddenly believe that your page is about umbrellas. However, if you place that metaphor in your page title, meta-description, H1 heading, and first paragraph of body copy, the search engine may lump you in with results for umbrellas.

Alignment across referral sites

Similar alignment needs to exist across referral sites. A referral site is any site that lets you list your business or nonprofit with a link back to your website. These sites generally ask for the same kind of information you've already created – namely, a title and description. As I said in my introduction, I'm not going to list specific technologies or sites where you can list your business because I want to focus on principles. Just run a search for "places to list my website," and you'll get the hottest spots today to freely list (a.k.a. manually index) your website.

The best method for creating these listings for both alignment and efficiency is to simply cut and paste your title and description. You may run into character count issues, so be prepared to edit down to the essentials.

Alignment across content

Aligned content across media types – website, blog, video, or social accounts – helps direct prospective customers to your content as they move among channels. Whether an interested prospect sees your ad, watches a video, or reads a blog article, their confidence in your brand grows with consistency and diminishes with inconsistency. This doesn't mean that every piece of collateral looks and sounds exactly the same. It simply means that you maintain consistent and aligned talking points for people and consistent keywords for search engines.

Alignment across links

Links are what make the internet into the world-wide web, connecting the vast repository of content we've posted to connected servers. As a digital marketer, you directly control some very important links. These include internal links within your site and marketing collateral, external links in advertisements you pay for, and external links from email or message campaigns. An inventory of all the links you create should reveal consistency in form and language.

Alignment across prospects

Big tech is getting smart at profiling people seemingly on its own. While search engines are busy indexing websites and webpages, internet services involved in advertising and marketing (often the same companies) are indexing users. They are busy building more and more exact profiles on internet visitors to understand what they're interested in. That profile allows them to connect users to sites based on interest. If you've misled search engines, or cast too broad a net, you'll miss out on the most interested prospects.

CONVERT

Alignment in the conversion phase of the customer journey is no less important than in the attract phase. The difference here is that it takes on a less technical aspect and a greater consideration of the buying process. Since we already have the interested prospect's attention, now is the time to build on that attention with content that reinforces the points that first attracted them and help them build a solid support for their purchasing consideration. As the digital marketer, you get to map out this path for the customer journey. You present options and signposts to guide them to content they need.

Align on established interest

Alignment during conversion is about presenting a united front to the customer. Your guidance should always align with the core points of interest that brought them to you in the first place. For example, if you know that your lead responded to ads about cost savings, a pathway for cost-conscious buyers needs to be presented to them. If the buyer responded to messaging about top-quality manufacturing, their buyer's journey needs to follow a pathway that builds value while reinforcing the top-quality manufacturing message.

This goes back to our discussion about emotional connection being the primary connection. By continuing to reinforce emotional connection while introducing other value-building benefits, you reinforce the buying decision.

Align on tone

The tone of the material in the customer journey also needs to follow the tone the customer started on. If your company story is based on friendly invitation, don't throw in a hard-hitting piece of collateral warning about the dangers that will befall customers who don't buy the product. Customers were attracted not only to a message, but to the tone or personality of that message. In most companies, the digital marketing team is not responsible for the tone of messaging, but they are responsible for finding ways to keep people on the path to becoming a customer. As a digital marketer, you need to notice – and gather data to support – when collateral in the journey is out of alignment and will derail the customer conversion process.

Segue to supporting content

You can think of the customer journey as someone wanting to take a trip and then planning that trip. Let's say someone has heard that Zion National Park might be a good place to visit. They may start with a web search. At this point, they are attracted but not sold. They are a lead – anonymous or otherwise. They want to know about the activities they might do there. Some of the activities appeal to them. Now they want to know if they can really make this happen, so they start looking at where they might stay while they are there and how much that would cost. They are no longer just attracted. They are building a supporting argument for being able to make a trip to Zion National Park.

As the digital marketer in this scenario, you are the one who makes it easy to access all the information the user might need to build a full picture of what making a purchase looks like. You present the links as well as the context or labels that explain why the links are there. You provide the cohesive picture of how to gather the necessary information.

RETAIN

Alignment never ends – the journey from customer to repeat customer to evangelist is as prone to attrition as the attraction and conversion journey. Consider ways digital marketing can apply alignment to retaining customers. Similar to determining a particular prospects path through the information gathering phase of conversion, we can use areas of interest shown by the customer to reenforce their continued interest and even growth as a customer. You may know from early interactions with a customer that they have interest in automating their business processes. As new products and features become available, that bit of data can be used to identify them as prime candidates for inclusion in current customer campaigns related to business automation. Or perhaps, you post an article on business automation on your blog, they might be included on a special email about the article.

Digital marketing has the ability to make customers feel special by tracking their specific interests, industries, or needs and pushing special outreach campaigns tailored to them. Anyone paying attention to the marketing industry has come across account-based marketing (ABM) and knows how difficult it can be outside of businesses that deal with just a few large customers. Within your customer base, however, you have a much better shot at getting close to ABM because you know what your customers have bought or continue to buy.

The job of digital marketing doesn't end after the customer buys. It's likely that many of your website visitors are your own customers looking for information. Customer satisfaction should be a big concern, and your site can play a huge part in building that customer satisfaction as long as it aligns with your customers' needs. Many companies silo their customers in a community site developed separately from the acquisition marketing going on in the marketing department. Here in customer communities, they develop messaging and thought leadership topics with little if any input from the marketing people that brought the customer on this journey. These community sites become an extension of customer support, full of dry documentation that lacks any of the tone and personality the customer experienced in their marketing journey. It's like being wined and dined during recruitment only to receive rations of bread and water on the job.

The main thing that should change from conversion to retention is the expressed sense of inclusion. The term "valued customer" needs to be at the forefront of every interaction with the customer. This genuine feeling of inclusion needs to be shared and felt. One of the best ways to feel included is to feel known. Do your customers feel like you know who they are? During the attraction and conversion phases of marketing, you learned quite a bit about them. Hopefully you retained that information in some intelligent and easy-to-recall way. Now you can mine that treasure trove of customer data to help them feel understood and valued.

During this phase, you can grow your relationship with the customer by using the information you shared with them during conversion to understand their interests. Do you know what they downloaded or received? Do you know what aspects of your offering most appealed to them? Do you have mechanisms for quantifying their interests beyond just industry and company size?

Let's say you run a bike supply site, and everything your loyal customer Sven has ever looked at or purchased is about mountain biking. Why would you make Sven feel unseen by sending him a promotional email about road bike tires?

Just like you were able to align advertising to activity and interest during the attraction phase, you can do the same during the retention phase – only much more efficiently.

Keeping promises
In the same way you maintain consistent references to the emotional connection in your materials as you move from attracting prospects to converting leads, you need to maintain that same connection in your customer satisfaction campaigns. Campaigns need to recognize why people bought your product and then remind them that you are still delivering that promised value.

It's all too easy in our customer communications to focus solely on meeting requests and touting product improvements. It's essential that you continue to remind them of the value they signed up for and how you continue to deliver that every day. It might be as simple as saying, "In addition to the personal-touch customer care our offices provide to patients, we are now offering...." Reminding customers about the value doesn't just enhance satisfaction and reduce attrition, it hands them the talking points they need to evangelize your business. When they remember the emotional connection that brought them to you in the first place, they are more likely to talk positively about your business and their relationship with you.

Summary
A campaign and content need to align across their various parts so the whole thing can maintain its veracity both to search engines and in the minds of prospective customers. Understand the customer and ensure that first and foremost content influences *them*. You need to align with stories people tell within the company so that people within the company rally behind the campaigns you present. The digital marketer can see

and create alignment across content presented to the customer during the different stages of marketing.

In the attraction stage, you need to maintain alignment along five main areas:
- Organic search
- Referral sites
- Content
- Links
- Prospects

During lead conversion, align with the core points of interest that brought them to you in the first place – the established interest. Material also needs to follow the tone the customer first encountered. The digital marketer makes it easy for leads to access all the information they might need to build a full picture of what making a purchase looks like.

In the retention stage, make customers feel special by tracking their specific interests, industries, or needs and pushing special outreach campaigns tailored to them. The main thing that should change from conversion to retention is the expressed sense of inclusion. To maintain alignment during this stage, campaigns need to recognize why people bought your product and then remind them that you are still delivering that promised value.

CHAPTER FOUR

Breadth

When the internet first popped up, it felt like a single marketing channel. People put up basic websites, linked pages built just in HTML with just a few "optimized" images – because images loaded slowly over dial-up. It was a pioneer endeavor with most people lacking formal education about web development, because so little was available. The first website I built for a client was built by looking at the source HTML of other sites to figure out how to make my client's site look the way they wanted. It contained no style sheets or JavaScript, both in their infancy. No backend database waited to be hacked. It was about as simple as a series of brochures linked together. The company thought of it as one marketing channel that sat alongside their mailing campaigns or their highway billboards.

Today's digital marketing covers a range of marketing channels. And just like in traditional advertising, where customers consume a variety of marketing channels such as TV ads, radio ads, billboards, newspaper, magazines, and even direct mail, the digital world has its own breadth of media types to consider.

Customers move around

In any given day, I see ads on search engine pages, receive offers by email, see ads during free online videos, and see promotional content on social sites and news sites. Many of these ads will be on the same or similar topics. Just like a traditional marketing campaign would run television, radio, magazine, newspaper, billboard, and direct mail campaigns, digital marketing needs to reach people across a wide swath of media to find them where they are.

Targeting a single channel or media type limits your results. If you focus on a single media type, you will only reach, with any meaningful frequency, the people who prefer that media type. This is because people, most people anyway, do not engage in just one activity.

Understanding media types and channels

Media types and channels, like products, have key demographics of people who listen, watch, or read them. If you are going to post ads on a video streaming service, you need to know how that service skews. If you know a channel participation skews toward younger men, that is not the place to promote a product primarily of interest to older women.

This applies as much to business-to-business products as to consumer products. The buyers you are dealing with have preferences about the media they consume to make decisions about products.

Media preferences may change at different stages of the buyer's journey. You also need to consider what that buyer needs to further sell your product into their organization. The main buyer may be persuaded by a series of in-depth white papers. However, in garnering support with their organization, they may need to send around a short demo video to coworkers who aren't as interested in the fine details, yet still hold sway on the decision.

What makes sense?

Breadth is about making sure you cover all the channels that make sense for your audience. And efficiency of breadth is making sure you don't waste time on channels or media types your buyers don't care about.

Early in my career, I took a job selling printing. It was one of the best experiences in my preparation for marketing. I made thousands of sales calls and managed dozens of client accounts, selling the same ink and paper as every other printer. But this story isn't about me. During that time, I got a print job from a client, a marketing director at a small group of restaurants. He had put together a customer newsletter that would be placed at the front counters of the restaurants. He wanted us to print the newsletter. The monthly newsletter ran about six months before he stopped running it. Apparently, people grabbing a taco for lunch didn't want to read newsletters about tacos. Who knew?

The point is that testing isn't bad, but continuing with something that isn't working is bad. Try lots of things, minimize or eliminate what doesn't work.

Attract

Since the dawn of advertising, promoters of products have known that good advertising needs to be seen often. Prospects need to see your brand with enough frequency to build memory connections. In TV advertising, we would accomplish this with baseline target rating points (TRP). Ordering a TV ad buy at 900 TRP means 90% of the target demographic sees the ad 10 times during the ad run. A typical target for something P&G or Pepsi might run. For today's digital marketer, it's still a matter of getting in front of a big enough percentage of your target market with enough frequency to move the needle. This means you run video, blog articles, social media billboards, and so on. Consider the breadth of media and channel options before you and the content needed for that media. Sometimes it might feel like a shotgun approach. When it does, refer to the alignment principle.

The breadth of media to consider during the attraction stage is different than the other stages. In the attraction stage, your prospect doesn't know you yet and will be unwilling to spend more than a few seconds to decide if they want to get to know you. Your ask or call to action at this phase is small – click to a landing page, look at our Amazon listing, download a coupon, etc.

Inline text ads

When we think of digital advertising, the inline text ad that comes up above search results is probably the most common. It was one of the first ways that search engine sites started to monetize their services and the effectiveness of the practice has kept it alive and well. It gives you the ability to create a variety of ads, each tied to specific search queries. The ads also give you the opportunity to test a variety of messages to see what resonates.

Like any digital ad, links should go to landing pages or blog articles aligned with the messaging of the ad, and you should have enough intelligence built into the link to gather meaningful information about the origin of the link and perhaps some of the interests of the viewer.

Payment models for this type of ad vary from pay per click to pay per view (what I call pay per display). I'm more a fan of the former, though I also like to know how many times an ad is displayed and not clicked. With most pay-per-click models, you set a budget for monthly spend, and when you hit that budget, the ad is no longer displayed. Ad pricing varies based on the popularity of the search terms your ad targets, but you know upfront what those costs will be. You'll know up front how many clicks you'll be able to get for the budget you set.

Webpages

I know we are quite a way into the book at this point and I've been referring to webpages throughout. The fact is that in the attract phase, the webpage is mostly the second step, the place people land after the initial call to action has been accepted. The main exception to this is in organic search. With organic search, like inline text ads, the prospect sees a heading and a description followed by a link. It's like a free little ad that you get to optimize. The place you optimize it is on your webpage. The title is your page's meta-title, and the description is your page's meta-description. You should craft these with as much care as you would your paid advertising.

Banner ads

Banner ads are like the magazine ads or billboards of the internet. They sit alongside the content users actually came to see or along the journey prospects are currently taking. They may be related to the site they're on, or they may have nothing to do with what the viewer is consuming. With today's intelligence around users, these ads can get very specific in who they target.

As someone who uses Adobe products and visits Adobe websites, ads for Adobe products and conferences follow me around the internet. I've also noticed ads for client companies following me for a while after I've searched for information about them. I know I could avoid all this by using incognito for my browsing, but what would be the fun in that. I kind of like seeing ads for motorcycle gear while reading articles on marketing metrics.

Because banner ads are static and easily overlooked, like billboards, they need a high frequency with the target audience to be effective. The billboards you pass on a road trip aren't nearly as impactful as the ones you pass on your daily commute.

Unlike printed billboards you see along the highway, banner ads can be changed up quickly and cheaply. Using a variety of ads gives you the opportunity to test messaging and imagery to see what works the best. This isn't something so easily done in a magazine ad or a TV commercial. You also have the opportunity to align ads with prospects more likely to be interested by engaging advertising technologies that use viewer profiles to decide what to deliver. Multiple technologies offer the kind of intelligence that improves the likelihood you are pitching your product to an interested person.

Banner ads should target a landing page or blog article and allow you to gather intelligence about the prospect who clicked on it, as well as the source it came from. Essentially, you want to hone your technology around intelligence gathering so you can determine how and why people find you.

Like inline text advertising, banner ads can be pay per click or pay per display, with the associated payment plans. Similarly, these ads are running on sites based on the site content or the user profile. You can also choose to advertise directly with certain sites.

A variation on the banner ad that captures attention is the cinemagraph. Cinemagraphs are banner ads with subtle movement added. This requires some advanced skills in image and video manipulation but can be a refreshing change from static banners. Let me be clear that I am not talking about animated GIFs. The movement loops about every 10 seconds or so and gives the image a feeling that calls attention to it. The animation is usually a subtle part of the overall piece, like grass moving in a breeze or a crosswalk light in the background changing from don't walk to walk. Text or graphics are laid over the image like you might do on a banner ad.

Video advertising

Video advertising on streaming channels has a lot more intelligence to it than the old TV advertising model that relied on TV program demographics aligned with TRP. Video advertising, like banner ads has the ability to target viewers based on user interest data. For example, a streaming channel might know that a user watches a lot of golf-related videos and serve up golf-related ads even during other news or lifestyle videos. One downside to streaming video ads is that they may also include the ability to skip the ad after a number of seconds. This data can also be useful because it can tell you about the engagement quality of your ads. I use the term engagement rather than entertainment, because although I'm a big fan of making ads entertaining, not every subject calls for it. There is nothing entertaining about ads for St. Jude's Children's Research Hospital, but I find them very engaging. Getting continuously skipped may mean you need to increase the engagement value or shorten the ad.

Short video

Short video is the brief-demonstration-of-value video that shares something about a product or service. These can sometimes be as long as five minutes, though tracking audience engagement will help you find your sweet spot. A software company I recently worked with started out with short videos around five minutes then after gathering some intelligence on viewer behavior, shortened these types of videos to under three minutes.

The short video is something you present at the conversion stage on a website page or campaign landing page, though during the attraction stage, they also work well as stand-alone content on social media and streaming sites. The idea is to pique interest and invite the viewer to learn more. You might also use short videos in a series to explain aspects of a more complex product or service, like a software system, but these would also be used more during the conversion stage.

Infographic

The infographic is a brief information piece that, like the short video, demonstrates value in a fun, graphical way. Depending on the content it may be useful at either the attraction or the conversion stages of the prospect's journey. Unlike something like a blog article, the infographic relies on quick, graphical representations to get attention and generate interest. These can be presented on a landing page or used as expandable images on social media sites. Companies often use them to illustrate a principle in a blog article allowing them to be further shared through other social and sharing sites.

External articles

The external blog article is a golden piece of digital marketing collateral, because it's posted by someone else and points back to you. Depending on the blog it's posted on, it may come with a wealth of information about the person who reads it, whether they click through to your site or not. You have to decide how to best use this information, whether it's to establish a relationship with the person or just tuck it away as a point of interest for the next time they come up on your radar. Even if the publisher doesn't have or share information about readers, you have a backlink to your site that tells search engines about the importance of the page that link goes to. The backlink is something that Larry Page, a founder of Google, considered to be an important aspect in ranking webpages.

Convert

During the conversion phase, you get more targeted and more detailed. The prospects have already indicated their interest and shown you some of their content consumption preferences. Don't take them for granted. Refer them to other content types as well. Your initial contact may be sold having watched the video, but her boss, the one holding the purse strings, wants to see some in-depth articles and a couple case studies before approving the purchase. Remember, you are never just creating that initial emotional connection, you are also arming the lead with the ammunition she needs to defend her purchase choice to others. When you buy that new set of touring skis, you know that somebody is going to ask why you bought that brand.

Another consideration of digital collateral during the conversion stage is the involvement of sales. In a long sales cycle, how can digital assets such as landing pages with linked collateral be used by a sales team to further an interested lead's progress toward purchasing. You need to be ready to share, preferably in some automated fashion, all the collateral consumed by the lead, so the sales team is not sending them duplicate information. On the flip side, sales needs to be letting you know what they find out about digital assets consumed by or sent to the lead, so you know what's being used and what's less helpful. This is also an important part of some later principles such as review, iteration, and curation.

Website

The website is the hub of the digital marketer's connection to leads during the conversion stage. The website with its carefully linked pages is a perfect laboratory for building effective content pathways that lead through a series of calls to action. Corporate sites are expected to be a source for all information needed about a company's products and methods of doing business. Every principle of digital marketing applies to building and effectively using your website. It is both a place to distribute information and to gather intelligence.

As a vital business hub, responsibility for the website falls to several stakeholders. It starts with IT who makes sure that it is both secure and robust enough to handle business demands. Operations has a part in the website, especially if it is used to conduct transactions. Corporate governance and legal have a stake in making sure website activity complies with local, state, and national regulations, as well as accurately portraying the nature of the business. Human resources often uses the website as part of its recruiting outreach.

Although all these stakeholders interact with and rely on the website, digital marketing is nearly always the keeper of the website. This is because the primary reason companies invest in websites is to drive revenue. Make sure you have a clear picture of the revenue function of your website and its place in converting customers. If it isn't doing that, it isn't living up to company expectations.

Many technologies and content management systems can help you build robust websites with solid tracking built in. Like any technology, you should only deploy a technology for your site after you know what you want it to do. Too often, sites are built on templates that don't allow for the unique advantages of the business and clutter the site with unnecessary pages and widgets that don't promote the company's needs. Three criteria that go into any content system you choose are:

1. How secure is it?
2. How easy is it to update content?
3. How easy is it to gather custom data?

I'm certain that consulting any of the dozens of authoritative works on building modern websites can help you expand on technical details, but these are the foundational pieces that need to be in place.

Emails

At the very least, if a salesperson hasn't been engaged with a prospect in the conversion phase, you should work to get the prospect's email address and start engaging them in an email campaign focused on their points of interest. Like any other piece of collateral, every email you send should offer something of value to the prospect in their quest for the best solution or benefit.

Consider the frequency of your emails according to the situation. If a user dropped off in the middle of an insurance quote form, their purchase might have some urgency, and daily e-mails could be warranted. If they watched a webinar for a product with a three- to six-month sales cycle, you might want to back it off to weekly emails. An important aspect to outreach communication is the timing of the initial communication. Leads contacted the same day after sharing their contact information have a higher conversion rate than leads contacted later. Interestingly, unless a contact was requested, contacting within 30 minutes lowers engagement – and maybe even comes off as a little creepy.

Blog articles

Although I often think of blog articles as something people read after they're attracted to a product or service, they do straddle the line between the attract and convert stages of marketing. The main reason I say they straddle the line is that they can be used as a target for an online ad campaign. You can say that for just about any of the pieces of the media you build for the conversion stage.

Blog articles provide the opportunity to tackle topics in a less formal way than you might in more static pieces of content like white papers or brochures. You can set up bios of regular writers who lend expertise on the topic while providing nuggets of value for the lead to add to their growing list of reasons to buy. Creating a range of writers who write from different disciplines or points of view gives you an additional layer of breadth in your digital marketing.

Blog articles can also be a great attractor for SEO, so be sure the associated meta-title and meta-description are working to attract your target audience.

Data sheets

Data sheets are those benefit and feature listing documents that customers ask for to see if what they're interested in buying really checks all the boxes. They exist as sort of an informal proof to what they saw in shorter content or heard in an initial conversation. They also help leads know what they don't know about the product. If the product is a high-end software system, the user is going to expect a demo, and the data sheets are what they can use to ask intelligent questions during the demo. Although they are rarely the direct collateral for an ad or email, they should be liberally linked from website and landing pages.

E-books

E-books in marketing lingo are not digitally published books like a Kindle book. They are more like medium-length digital brochures designed to be read on a screen. They are generally laid out in a landscape format (wider than they are tall) and are highly graphical. This is another one of those line-straddling pieces, because it may be the collateral for a digital campaign in ads, email, or social media. E-books have the advantage over printed material of being sprinkled with links back to landing pages or other related content.

The most common use of the e-book is as a document that can be downloaded, making them highly portable for salespeople to share. Having a version that can be built into a webpage would also give the digital marketer the ability to gather intelligence on the behavior of prospects as they view the e-book.

White papers

A tried-and-true workhorse of the business-to-business, long-sales-cycle process, the white paper carries a lot of weight when properly used. I would be less likely to use it as a collateral piece for top-of-funnel advertising the way I might an e-book or a video, but it is highly sought after by professionals making big expenditures for their company. Getting into nitty-gritty details, the kind reserved for long-form documents like white papers, is the kind of due diligence expected of people making big purchases professionally.

In the digital marketing practice, white papers are linked from webpages and other collateral. When I want to say more in an e-book or a blog article, but I'm not sure how interested the customer is, I reference a white paper where all the details are kept. The intelligence gathered from this click through also tells me about the interest level of the prospect.

Long videos

Long videos can be broken into a couple of categories. First, a long demonstration or product tour, and second, a webinar or panel discussion. These are generally longer than a short video and may last as long as an hour. Running a long demonstration or webinar as a scheduled event gives you the opportunity to gather some user information, such as name, email, and possibly company. Long videos can be a great indicator of interest. Drop off rates can also help you determine not just interest, but where the video might be lacking engaging content.

Case studies

The case study is an interesting piece of digital collateral because, while it is essential for later-stage companies, it can be very hard to produce in early-stage companies. Don't consider the case study to be essential to your early-stage company. The vision and authenticity of your other marketing collateral will carry the day. Visionary or early adopters are looking to make their own decision about how the product or service will benefit them. Later-stage companies facing early majority customers are going to see a call for case studies as they start running into buyers who are only willing to buy if they can see how the product benefitted someone else like them. At later stages, much of your growth is coming from word of mouth and brand development inertia, rather than the targeted digital marketing campaigns being talked about here. For more on the stages of growth and marketing see Geoffrey Moore's books, *Crossing the Chasm* and *Inside the Tornado*.

Marketing stages aside, used at the right time, relevant customer stories linked to webpages and other collateral can help add credence to messaging about your product or service. As you consider case studies to link to a campaign, page, or other collateral, make sure the case study aligns with the interests of the group you are targeting in the campaign. If you're running a campaign about your new rowing machine, you probably don't want to link a testimonial about your stationary bike.

Retain

Approach customer satisfaction, upsell, and upgrade campaigns with the same amount of breadth as you would your other campaigns. Perhaps it's because these things are handled by different departments, but the breadth of media delivered during these campaigns usually only takes advantage of one or two of the available media types.

Customers may not actively research the product once they are using it, so helping them get the most from the product requires concerted campaigns with the same breadth of content you provided to prospects. Something that changes is the tone of how the collateral is presented. These people are now in the club – loyal users enjoying the benefits of the product. Invitations to make additional investments in your product or service need to acknowledge that inclusion across a breadth of media. Simply reusing marketing material designed for prospects, may leave your customers feeling like outsiders – like you don't see them.

Recognize them as champions of the product

Creating a repeat customer and an evangelist requires tightly targeted campaigns that help them see how they have continued to benefit and how they can champion the product with others like themselves. When customers see the value they are receiving from the product, they are more likely to share success stories. When sharing those success stories among your customer base, make sure to set the customer as the real hero of the story for using the product to their advantage. Set these stories in a wide range of content including videos, articles, e-books, and web pages.

Make stories sharable

As your customer base grows, digital marketing systems to request, manage, and distribute these success stories will be essential. Customers, even your most vocal evangelists, are busy. Make sharing media easy for them. This is also an opportunity for customers to help you achieve breadth of distribution. Content should include quick links to share across top social and sharing sites. Adding these links also adds traceability to what gets shared and to what channels. Obviously your tracking will never be a hundred percent with downloadable content, but with your own links, you'll be able to better gauge trends.

Give customers control

What about the dreaded opt out we are required to provide for email communication? Rather than making customer communication an all or nothing, create levels of communication. We can do this both according to types of content – updates, offers, alerts – as well as by media type preferences – video, e-books, email. This allows both for customers to receive content in their preferred media type as well as informing your data about media preferences.

By giving customers control over the types and frequency of the marketing messages they receive from you, you're letting them know you respect their time and don't want to fill up their in box with things they don't want. When customers do engage in setting their contact preferences, don't let this live in a silo. Integrate this information with the other intelligence you have on the customer. Digital marketing should have a growing profile on each customer that can be used to inform campaigns, as well as inform support, about the customer's activity and disposition.

Make sharing easy to navigate

Another way to make sharing easy is to categorize and label collateral for your customer to select from. Just dropping your customer into an alphabetical list of resources will lead to less-than-optimal results. If you give them a logical way to select the collateral that fits the friend they are sharing with, even including brief descriptions of collateral, you increase the likelihood that their friends will receive something that resonates with them.

SUMMARY

Today's digital marketing covers a range of marketing channels, and the digital world has its own breadth of media types to consider.

Targeting a single channel or media type limits your results.

Media preferences may change at different phases of the buyer's journey.

Efficiency of breadth is making sure you don't waste time on channels or media types your buyers don't care about.

The breadth of media to consider during the attraction phase:
- Inline text ads
- Webpages
- Banner ads
- Video advertising
- Short video
- Infographic
- External articles

The breadth of media to consider during the conversion phase:
- Website
- Emails
- Blog articles
- Data sheets
- E-books

- White papers
- Long videos
- Case studies

Four strategies that rely on breadth of content in your customer retention marketing

- Recognize them as champions of the product
- Make stories sharable
- Give customers control
- Make sharing easy to navigate

CHAPTER FIVE

Depth

Think binge watching. Depth of content can be engaging, and it can also be expensive. The expense comes when you want to make sure your depth of content isn't more of the same. Think of your depth of content like a learning path that leads somewhere. It takes writers capable of creating a story arch to lead the customer along a meaningful path and a digital marketing team that can capture leads and manage the pathways through the content. Knowing what the customer needs to know next isn't a one and done process. You'll need to rely on an iteration process that I'll be going into in a chapter on the principle of iteration. Except in very small companies, creating content often falls outside the purview of the digital marketer. That said, as a digital marketer, you need to understand the targeting, timing, delivery, and tracking associated with deep content. You also need to understand that the team will look to you to find and fill gaps in the customer journey.

Targeting

Presenting a particular path for a prospect or customer relies on the target analysis work you've already done. What media helped the customer most in their investigation of your offering? What supported their decision to buy? When was the "aha" moment where they knew this was the product for them? How much more did they investigate after the moment? What helped them on-board others in the decision? What else would have helped them? How much did information from outside sources influence their decision?

These questions represent consumption activities by customers who chose to buy what you are selling. They help identify the depth of information needed to decide. Did you provide enough depth to meet customer needs? Do you have more content than you need to meet customer needs? Is your content on target or does it stray into areas target customers don't care about?

Timing

Timing can be time based, though it's more likely to be event based. You want to reach out to a customer with the right level of detail when they're ready for it. Some prospects are actively searching, while other may have dropped into your site and made some notes to plan their due diligence that may not start until next month or next quarter. Slow progress doesn't mean a prospect isn't interested; it may just mean that different factors are at work in their case when compared to a faster moving client.

A lot about timing depends on the buyer's point in their own journey. As a college student, I remember spending weeks deciding on the right mountain bike. The money represented months of savings from my meager income, and I didn't want to make the wrong decision. Today, if I decided I needed a new mountain bike, I would have one in a day or two. Several factors are at play here. First, I know more about mountain bikes and what I want and need. Second, a bike now represents a smaller investment as a percentage of my income and therefore a smaller investment as a percentage of time to research.

Consider that every customer is not at the same level in their readiness to buy, and plan accordingly how much you push them to deeper marketing content.

Continually Invite

Delivery should meet the needs of the customer and stick to proven sales processes. What I mean by this is that customers need content to make decisions, but you also need to encourage them to make decisions, even if it's just a decision to investigate further.

At the heart of every piece of collateral should be an invitation, a call to action. From a content creation perspective, this should be defined even before the content is created. Creating content and considering a call to action as an afterthought is like buying a trailer before you know what you need it to carry. In marketing, content is the trailer that delivers the invitation, not the other way around. It is the framework that supports and influences the acceptance of the call to action.

You can think of your digital marketing path as a series of steppingstones that each invite a person to take the next step. I like to create flowchart visuals that show the path with each of the invitations listed to see if I have gaps in the invitations I'm presenting. Am I asking for too much too early or am I not asking for enough when the lead is clearly interested? Early on, these are qualitative decisions. With additional data collection, they can become quantitative decisions.

Tracking

Wouldn't it be nice if buyers told you up front how they wanted to pursue their investigation of your product? But they don't, because for the most part they don't even know themselves. But you can find out by tracking their path through your content. By tracking where they go and when they go there, you can help later prospects and leads find the quickest path forward. This only works if you can track movement over time.

Tracking your prospects and leads, and even customers of that matter, through their product investigations requires preparation on your part. You need to build in mechanisms that can not only tell you what they looked at, but the chronology in which they looked at it.

Technology exists to help you do this, but you need to know what you want to know before you engage in tools to provide that information. You need to gather rudimentary information and understand what you will actually use in your efforts to create the right amount of depth before you open the flood gates of data that such tools generally offer. Before you start basking in the hundreds of available data metrics, you need to know the five that matter most to your business.

The buyer's perspective

Although all content and learning paths need to be considered from the buyer's perspective, no place in your content needs to reflect the buyer's perspective more than your frequently asked questions. Have you ever gone to company's FAQ with a question only to find nothing but softball questions that give them an opportunity to tout only their strengths? When you get into the more detailed content about your product, like an FAQ page, are you presenting content that answers questions prospective customers have or are you just answering questions you like the answers to?

Who knows what buyers actually want to know? In long sales deals, salespeople and sales engineers who demonstrate the product know. Customer support and, in some companies, implementers know. Customers know. And you want to know who else knows? Your competitors. This is one place that competitive research can add value in your processes. Answers about your product that can be distorted by your competitors definitely need to be addressed within your detailed content. As they say in politics, "Control the narrative."

Attract

During the attraction phase, content needs to be short and easily consumable. This doesn't mean that you can't create depth. Depth at the attraction stage comes in the form of variety. Variety offers you the opportunity to create frequency without being overly repetitive. This is especially important in social media.

A strategy I recommend for posting across social channels, is to write about 60 variations of your message to get you through a month of posts. Yes, 60, at least. That's only 3 a day 5 days a week for 4 weeks. If you don't have someone who has written for high-volume campaigns, this might seem daunting at first. But you aren't writing long content. These are not 60 blog articles. These are 60 blurbs that promote your longer content or in some cases send people straight to a store or purchase page. If you need to start slower to get your creative juices flowing, start with 10 pieces and cycle through them while you ramp up by adding more to your library.

With graphical content like banner ads, infographics, and memes, you can expand the ways you can vary your content, as you make frequent posts or ad buys in social media and paid search advertising. You can use different visual elements – images or illustrations – along with the same text or change up the text on the same design. Creating variations allows you to create depth within individual media types.

Use series and echoes

In TV and radio advertising an echo advertisement is generally a 15 second ad that is a continuation or "echo" of a longer 30 second ad. You can do the same thing in social media. By creating a series of ads along the same style and theme, you bring the earlier ads to mind, reinforcing their influence. Delivery can get tricky because unlike TV, where you control delivery on certain channels and shows, you have less control about the order in which people see your content on social media.

This means you have to be smart about when you release pieces by giving enough time for the early content to run its course before posting echoes or next-in-series pieces.

Convert

Much of my discussion of depth at the start of this chapter referred to the lead conversion stage. Rather than go over all the same points I already covered, I'd like to dive into a topic that can create an unnecessary drain on your content creation resources. A concept that's been popular for some time now is to split the conversion stage into two separate stages – nurture and convert. The concept seems to be that leads who show interest but are not ready to buy should be nurtured until they are ready to buy. I don't subscribe to this school of thought because I believe it runs contrary to the fundamental purpose of marketing – to create a customer.

Earlier in this chapter, I wrote about continually inviting. If you are continually inviting, you are converting. You may be converting slowly, but you are still converting. The concept of nurturing to me seems like asking someone to walk in place for a while and puts you at risk of creating more content than necessary. If you have a bunch of content designed to help a lead stay where they are or walk in place, you have to spend time and money to create it, review it, iterate it, and curate it without seeing economic benefit from it.

Make each step meaningful

Each step in the conversion stage comes with a call to action that helps the buyer take a step closer to buying. If you find that you lose a lot of people at the same place in the process, then take a look at perhaps breaking that big step into more incremental steps or analyzing it for an information gap, but don't create a holding pattern. Even slow progress is progress. Holding patterns in your conversion process have real costs.

Your market is too vast and your competition too aggressive to spend resources on people who aren't ready to move forward.

Before you send me your story of the client who you nurtured and ended up with a great deal, let me remind you that I too was in sales, and I too have nurture success stories. But that is sales. It costs very little for a salesperson to nurture a lead with an occasional email, phone call, or a stop by the office when they're in the area. But that prospective buyer cannot be the target of marketing campaigns that consume resources better used to influence leads who are progressing.

I know this is a point of controversy, and I know a lot of content marketers make a very good living feeding the nurture space. I also know that at the end of the day the total cost of marketing has to be amortized across the number of customers created and that cost, along with the amortized sales expense, become the customer acquisition cost or CAC. The higher the CAC, the longer it takes to reach profitability on a per customer basis. And per customer profitability roles up into company profitability. In other words, big things are made up of lots of little things, and keeping leads making meaningful steps forward is one of those little things that leads to big success.

Retain

How much depth is required to retain customers? Companies like Adobe and Salesforce spend millions of dollars on conferences designed to increase their customer's depth of knowledge about the product. They bring in experts, give massive seminars, hold in-depth workshops, and generously wine and dine current customers to make sure they get the deepest product knowledge possible. What are they doing on the digital front? The same thing. They are providing avenues to promote, answer questions about, and rally customers to greater appreciation for the products they sell.

You may not have the budget and resources of Adobe or Salesforce, but you do have access to the same internet and the same digital tools to influence customers and affect their affinity for your brand and products. At what level of expertise do customers begin to make value jumps with your product? What level of engagement with your product moves a customer from satisfied to evangelistic?

In working with customers at a software company, I began to notice a trend among users. I would ask them some basic questions to gauge their enthusiasm for the product. I would then ask them about their experience with some industry-specific features of the software. I followed that up with questions about their use of the built-in dashboards in the software. Even before I asked this question, I often knew the answer. Those that had answered unenthusiastically about the product hadn't started using the dashboards, while those with high enthusiasm for the product were actively using, building, or customizing dashboards. I began a customer satisfaction campaign to promote the use of dashboards among the customer base, because I wanted customers who weren't just satisfied, but evangelistic.

What aspects of your product absolutely delight customers, but often go underutilized? What additional learning pathways can you provide to customers to help them engage more fully with your product, service, or brand? How much depth is needed to turn ho-hum customers into evangelists?

Summary

Think of your depth of content like a learning path that leads somewhere. Presenting a path for a prospect or customer relies on the target analysis work you've already done. Reach out to a customer with the right level of detail when they're ready for it.

At the heart of every piece of collateral should be an invitation, a call to action. Think of your digital marketing path as a series of steppingstones that each invite buyers to take the next step.

Build tracking into your digital marketing that not only tells you what people looked at, but the chronology in which they looked at it.

In your detailed content, present answers to questions prospective customers actually have and not just answers to questions you like.

Depth at the attraction stage comes in the form of variety, which allows you to create frequency without being overly repetitive. Also consider using series and echoes.

If you are continually inviting, you are converting. Each step in the conversion stage comes with a call to action that helps the lead take a step closer to buying.

Questions to ask as you market at the retention stage include:
- What aspects of your product absolutely delight customers, but often go underutilized?
- What additional learning pathways can you provide to customers to help them engage more fully with your product, service, or brand?
- How much depth is needed to turn ho-hum customers into evangelists?

CHAPTER SIX

Review

If you've read even half a dozen books on success, you've likely come across the marshmallow study that left kids alone with a marshmallow and told them if they waited to eat the marshmallow until the adult returned, they would get a second marshmallow. Repeated tellings of the abbreviated story leave people thinking that all those who waited saw grand success in life and all those who ate the marshmallow became abject failures. To quote one retelling, children who waited ended up having "higher SAT scores, lower levels of substance abuse, lower likelihood of obesity, better responses to stress, better social skills as reported by their parents, and generally better scores in a range of other life measures."

Later replications of the experiment that accounted for more factors, such as home life, trust in the adult, and so on, found less correlation between the results and social problems, though the children who waited did tend to score higher on scholastic tests in later years. ("The marshmallow test: Bunkum or a true predictor of future success?")

Although the ability to delay gratification shows a higher tendency to succeed, the two groups of children have a large overlap on the success scale. Like many tendencies within a population, you can picture it as a bell curve where the x axis is success and y is the number of people at any given success point. If you split the curve with a vertical line according to the ratio of eaters and waiters and say the less successful part are the eaters and the more successful part are the waiters, you'll be misinterpreting the data. A more accurate depiction would be two bell curves overlaid, one for the eaters and one for the waiters. The waiters bell curve would sit a little to the right, toward the higher success end of the chart. The vast majority of both groups would overlap in the middle. Meaning that most of the preschoolers who ate the marshmallow turned out just fine.

The point is that data needs to be reviewed and revisited to update assumptions. You also need to consider the overlapping areas revealed by data. Not everything is black and white, and results can change over time. Or I should say, results will change over time.

Revisit assumptions

Although I've already touched on it a bit, review is a principle that runs throughout everything digital marketing touches. A central element of digital marketing is collecting data or intelligence. By contrast, review covers revisiting assumptions in the light of new data.

In review, you bring together stakeholders and digital marketers to produce a full picture of what's going on in digital marketing. As you look at the different metrics along each phase of the marketing process, you challenge assumptions based on the data and see how revised assumptions might change your strategies moving forward.

For example, you may have a land and expand model by geographies, and your top advertising draw might be hot drinks. As you expand your business southward, data might start showing that more customers are coming in for cold drinks. You need to adjust the offerings you lead with in your marketing in those areas. You've challenged an assumption about your customers and changed strategy to meet a new reality. This one may be obvious and maybe you could have guessed it. Most assumptions we challenge are not so easily sleuthed out, and many may be difficult to change as people cling to the things they've already invested in.

Does the thing that mattered most last year matter most today? If not, what matters most now?

Are the media channels that worked well to reach your customers last year as relevant today? If not, what channels do your prospects consume now? Has their preferred content medium changed? Is there a new content type that you should be investigating? Are aspects of the preferred content type changing, such as preference for shorter or longer videos?

How has your customer demographic changed? Are sales to your target industry dropping off, while sales in another industry are now growing? Maybe the loyalty you had among 20-somethings a decade ago has shifted to loyalty among 30-somethings, who now consume media differently than they used to.

A WORKABLE REVIEW PATTERN

For several years, I took time off every summer to staff a youth leadership camp. The gig was pretty light work for the adults on staff, because the program was youth led by former participants who spent the year leading up to the camp coalescing into a working staff. Each night during the event, we met together as a staff and reviewed the day. We went through each of the lessons, activities, and participant interactions for that day and assessed according to three criteria: stop, start, and continue.

Stop was assigned to things that just weren't getting us the results we wanted. Sometimes these were new things we were trying out, and other times they were things we had always done with smaller groups that just weren't working with bigger groups.

Start referred to things we needed to start doing to better meet our course objectives. It could be something as simple as a change we made on a particularly rainy week – "End lessons five minutes earlier to allow for putting on and taking off rain gear, as well as trudging through mud."

Continue meant that something was working, and we should keep doing it. This one may seem obvious, but failing to mention things that should continue might cause them to fall off everyone's radar or leave the impression they were being replaced by things we were starting.

This simple pattern adapts well to digital marketing review meetings. Data drives most of the decisions, though the experience of the team can lead to quality interpretations of that data.

Managing a group review

Keep your discussions and decisions tied to data. A few agenda-driven personalities in a group can turn a committee discussion into an exercise in group dynamics. In marketing meetings, you are dealing with multiple people whose whole stock in trade is the art of persuasion. They are trained and practiced at turning a room full of people to see things their way. However, consensus is not the same thing as correct. I've found that tabling unsupported decisions can keep a meeting progressing, while protecting the integrity of your data-driven review processes.

Assumptions and data

A wilderness experiment in assumptions that has been repeated and verified multiple times involves hiking cross country. A recent version of the experiment published in 2009 was conducted by Dr. Jan L. Souman of the Max Planck Institute for Biological Cybernetics in Tübingen, Germany.

While looking into multi-sensory perception, Dr. Souman led an experiment that tracked the movements of volunteers sent into both a German forest and a desert in Tunisia. When participants could see the sun or moon, they could walk in more or less a straight line. On cloudy days or nights with no moon, they circled back around, often several times. Dr. Souman pointed out that the brain appeared to be lacking a fundamental visual cue to help make sense of the jumble of other data it was receiving.

"The brain has different sources of information for almost everything," said Dr. Souman. "But all those information sources are kind of relative. They don't tell you you are moving in the same direction as an hour ago."

The sun or moon or a prominent landmark like a distant mountaintop seem necessary to provide cues and maintain a course. These findings align with observations by many back-country guides, rescuers, and hiking experts, who say that to avoid walking in circles, hikers should rely on a compass or a GPS, rather than themselves. ("Hiking Around in Circles? Probably, Study Says")

What is your fixed reference as you hike off into your review process with all its perceptions and assumptions? As you go through your review process, you want to make sure you have both your previous assumptions and most current data on hand. Write down assumptions behind your digital marketing strategy and revise as needed between reviews. If you rely simply on recollection, you may find the group a little fuzzy and discordant on strategy points as each has reinterpreted previous discussions. Keeping snapshots of assumptions, data, and decisions from meeting to meeting will aid in moving forward rather than repeatedly circling back to the same topics.

In the chapter on intelligence, I covered several areas regarding the types of data points you need to be collecting. These will change according to the type of business you are in and the unique advantages your business brings to the market. The data points and metrics reflect data captured over time from your customer interactions. They lay a foundation for the assumptions that drive your strategy. For example, you may find that customers are most likely to open marketing emails on Tuesday and Wednesday. Even though this became an underlying assumption in your email strategy, you need to continue to test and review it to make sure it is still the case.

Attract

As I go through the points of data collection for the attraction phase of marketing, you will see some redundancies with things I've mentioned earlier and some new items. I've gathered them all here to make it easier to reference. As I mentioned at the outset of the book, I haven't set out to create a how-to manual on assembling your digital marketing machine. So this list is by no means exhaustive. I expect that this will get your wheels turning on additional data points important in your specific business.

Prospect profile

The profile of your target prospect should be expressed as much as possible in terms of actionable data. Content creators may expand on this to help them understand the mind of the prospect, but for the purposes of digital marketing, you need to know certain things about them to reach them in the vast digital marketplace. These make up your assumptions about the target prospect and become a part of the data set challenged during reviews. Some key points here include:

- **Media preferences** – What is the hierarchy of media consumption by type of media?
- **Areas of interest** – What industries, jobs, hobbies, activities, or other areas of interest indicate possible content people may search for?
- **Times of interest** – When are they most likely to be searching in terms of times of day or days of the week?
- **Times of engagement** – When are they most likely to be actively making a decision to buy in terms of times of the week, month, or year?

Key metrics

> "A metric is a measuring system that quantifies a trend, dynamic, or characteristic."
>
> ~ *Marketing Metrics*

The art of turning data into metrics is the art of seeing the story behind the numbers. We often talk about telling your data story, though you'll create the most impactful story when you turn your data into a metric. For example, the number of new leads is an interesting data point, as is the amount of money the company spends attracting new leads. But cost per lead (new leads/attraction cost) is a metric with some muscle to build a strategy on. You can start considering how efficient your marketing, sales, and on-boarding process is and whether you can hone it a little more. It also hands a point of intelligence to the whole organization to help them discover when a customer becomes profitable. In a product company, it can even inform a better understanding of the price point a product needs to be at to be profitable.

Attraction metrics
- **Page views** – the number of requests to load (or reload) a single page of a website
- **Visits** – the number of times a user loaded at least one page on the website
- **Visitors** – the number of unique visitors to a website
- **Returning visitors** – the number of visitors who come back more than once
- **Visitor sources** – the location where visitors linked from to reach your site, including other sites, email, or direct input
- **Bounce rate** – the number of people who land on a page on your website, then leave without clicking on anything else or

visiting a second page on the site divided by the total number of visitors to your website, expressed as a percentage
- **Visitor conversion rate** – the number of conversions you achieve divided by the total number of visitors to your website, expressed as a percentage
- **Leads** – the number of prospects who click on a call to action
- **Cost per lead** – the cost of attraction stage digital marketing divided by the number of leads
- **Click-through rate** – the number of clicks that your ad receives divided by the number of times your ad is shown
- **Cost per click** – the overall cost of ads divided by the number of clicks the ads receive
- **Impressions** – the number of times a user opens an app or website and an advertisement is visible
- **Cost per thousand impressions** – the total amount paid for 1,000 impressions of an ad
- **Average frequency** – the average number of times a person is exposed to an advertisement within a schedule
- **Net reach** – the number of unique people exposed to an advertising message at least once within a given period of time over the total addressable target market, usually expressed as a percentage
- **Effective frequency** – the number of times a person must be exposed to an advertising message before a response is made
- **Effective reach** – the number of people or percent of population reached with frequency equal to or greater than effective frequency
- **Share of voice** – a measure of the market your brand owns compared to your competitors

CONVERT

Review of the conversion phase focuses on gaining a better understanding of the path the customer follows as they move from that first response to a buying decision. You can often learn vital information by also reviewing the path of those who chose not to buy. Similarities and trends here may show you gaps in your process or may point to a misalignment between your offering and the leads you attract.

Lead profile

- **Content preferences** – the types of media or specific subject areas the lead is interested in
- **Content depth** – the amount of or number of steps taken by the lead into the conversion content
- **Point of conversion** – the step in the conversion stage or amount of content consumption reached before choosing to buy
- **Point of abandonment** – the step in the conversion stage or amount of content consumption reached before choosing not to buy
- **Length of engagement** – the time spent in the conversion stage before making a buying decision
- **Purchasing engagement** – the time from decision to buy to completion of purchase

Conversion metrics

- **Customers** – the number of people who buy the product or service
- **Conversion rate** – the number of customers over the number of leads, expressed as a percentage

- **Customer acquisition cost** – the cost of marketing during a period divided by the number of new customers added during the period
- **Average order cost** – the cost of marketing during a period divided by the number of purchases made during that period
- **Abandoned purchases** – the number purchasing events that leads initiate but do not complete
- **Abandonment rate** – the number of abandoned purchases divided by the total number of purchasing events initiated, expressed as a percentage

Retain

Review in the retention stage focuses primarily on customer campaign response and lowering the churn or attrition rate. Customer support may often play a key role in understanding the customer and their difficulties. In small companies or when dealing with direct customer support people, discussions may slide into anecdotal evidence. Be sure to back up decisions in this area with data across the customer base.

Perceptions in customer satisfaction among people who deal one on one with customers don't always align with the aggregate view shown in data. When I was working with a wholesale company in the housewares space, we experienced a runaway success with a new product line. Customer support staff, who had typically dealt with calls about products selling by the tens of thousands or even hundreds of thousands, found themselves answering calls for a product line selling in the millions. While walking past customer service, I overhead a customer support representative say, "Oh yeah, those break all the time. I'll send you out a new one." Concerned, I made a point of having informal chats with people in customer service to get their take on the new product line. They liked the product but thought it had a lot of problems and broke all the time. They also thought we were going to have big problems with customer satisfaction.

The truth was that the product had one of the lowest defect rates of any electric product we sold. Great care had been taken in selecting good factories and setting up our own quality assurance testing at the factory site and at our warehouses. Our defect rates were well below industry standards, and our customer satisfaction rate was one of the highest in the industry. We had done extensive customer research and found that customers loved the product and the brand. More than 90% of those surveyed would recommend it to a friend.

The problem was that customer support only saw their total call volume increase because our total sales volume was ten times what they were accustomed to. We put up posters throughout the office and especially around customer support with customer quotes and data about how loved and successful the product was. Support reps shifted from saying, "Those break all the time," to saying, "That almost never happens. I'll send you out a new one." Internal perceptions don't always match data. Using them in place of data can be an expensive mistake.

Customer profile

The customer profile builds on profiles from the previous two stages and, for the purposes of digital marketing, adds data about customer outreach response.

Retention metrics

- **Customer outreach response rate** – the number of customer responses to a call to action divided by the number of impressions, expressed as a percentage
- **Customer retention rate** – the total of the number of customers at the end of a period less new customers added during the period divided by the number of customers at the beginning

of the period ((Customers end of period – new customers) / customers start of period)
- **Customer churn rate** – the total of the number of customers at the start of the year less the number of customers at the end of the year divided by the number of customers at the start of the year ((Customers start of year – customers end of year) / customers start of year)
- **Customer lifecycle duration** – the average length of time a customer continues with your product or service (generally used by service or recurring revenue businesses)

Summary

Data needs to be periodically reviewed and revisited to correct or update assumptions. Build a workable review plan around the structure of stop, start, and continue. Keep your discussions and decisions tied to data by tabling unsupported decisions until they are supported by data. Maintain a record of previous assumptions and most current data as fixed reference points to keep reviews from going around in circles. Use data to create metrics that help you see the story behind the numbers.

A key review point of the attraction stage should be the prospect profile which includes media preferences, areas of interest, times of interest, and times of engagement.

Attraction stage metrics
- Page views
- Visits
- Visitors
- Returning visitors
- Visitor sources
- Bounce rate
- Visitor conversion rate

- Leads
- Cost per lead
- Click-through rate
- Cost per click
- Impressions
- Cost per thousand impressions
- Average frequency
- Net reach
- Effective frequency
- Effective reach
- Share of voice

Conversion data points and metrics

A key review point of the conversion stage should be the lead profile which includes content preferences, content depth, point of conversion, point of abandonment, length of engagement, and purchasing engagement.

Conversion stage metrics include:
- Customers
- Conversion rate
- Customer acquisition cost
- Average order cost
- Abandoned purchases
- Abandonment rate

Retention data points and metrics

A key review point of the retention stage should be the customer profile which includes the customer outreach response.

Retention stage metrics include:
- Customer outreach response rate
- Customer retention rate

- Customer churn rate
- Customer lifecycle duration

CHAPTER SEVEN

Iteration

At first glance, review and iteration might look like the same thing. The issue that comes up when you group them together is that you can end up with teams that constantly review but never iterate. Or – and this may be more common – organizations that iterate without review. In which case, iteration becomes a marketing activity, rather than a strategic step forward. You can see this with organizations changing their branding with no visible ROI – often just a vanity project in the wake of leadership changes. These projects can derail other digital marketing activities while the digital marketing team shifts production cycles off to rebranding efforts.

On the other hand, visual branding changes that have a clear ROI become part of iteration for strategic advancement. Consider the example of American Express, who changed their logo a few years ago. Many people didn't even notice the change – but graphic designers noticed. American Express changed the box with a blue gradient to a box that is solid blue. The logo became much easier to use across all file types. When you consider the vast number of places the logo gets used, this little change likely paid for itself in short order. When you undertake iterations on brand changes, consider subtly changing it over time without disrupting your money-making activities.

Iterating your digital marketing comes in several forms. Probably the most common iteration I've run into is making changes to content to improve response rates within your target audience. You may also make incremental changes on the timing of digital campaigns, such as when they run and how long to follow up. You might iterate on technical aspects of the interaction with customers. What mechanisms do you use to reach out to customers? If they fill out a form, can you add more fields or remove some fields from forms to improve completion rates? Let's dive into these types of iterations and look at how you might strategically approach iteration in your organization.

Content iteration

I start here because of how often I see this as top of mind in marketing organizations. When you create an e-book, you've built something everyone in the organization can look at, consider, nit-pick, and likely improve on, and they do. In the meantime, those looking at the data are the ones who can provide the clearest answer on what's going on with the content. In one company I worked with, the head of channel sales complained that the illustrations in the latest catalog looked like clip art. He suggested the marketing team remove them. Data showed that since adding the illustrations, response rates had improved over collateral with the same content but no illustrations. Data trumped opinion. The illustrations stayed, though the comments prompted later iterating them to a more sophisticated style.

Content iteration can be squishy, especially in a healthy organization where people feel free to share their opinions about it. This is why establishing a data-driven purpose for every iteration is essential. Every iteration also needs to come with a cost-benefit analysis. Changing content takes time and that time costs money. Tracking the cost of the iterations and increase in activity generated is an essential part of making sure digital marketing is honing and advancing rather than just changing things up.

When someone says that the current marketing has gotten stale, the next question should be, "Stale to who (or whom – you choose)?" In digital marketing terms, this should mean that the customer is no longer responding to it. Maybe you've been running the same content in the same way for so long that it's become easy to ignore. If that is the case, then a change is warranted – an incremental change.

Have you noticed that GIECO cycles through different ad campaigns, but the gecko seems to always stick around? The gecko campaign simply gets iterated to keep it fresh because it works.

Timing Iteration

John Sculley, former CEO of Apple, quipped, "Timing is everything." And many have proposed that his amazing success was due to the timing he had of joining Apple just as Jobs' and Wozniak's creations became a market success.

Timing – though low cost and easy to measure – goes relatively unchanged in most digital campaigns, while companies throw gobs of money at content changes. What time does your system send out e-mails? Is there a prime time of the year or month to run a campaign? What day of the week will you see the biggest response to your outreach?

I generally play golf on Saturdays, not every Saturday, but that's usually the best time to get together with friends. Whether I play well or I play poorly, on Sunday and Monday, I'm thinking about golf. And Monday is the day I'm most likely to go to the range to fix whatever aspect of my game wasn't working on Saturday. For me, the time that I'm most likely to listen to a message about golf is Saturday night to Monday afternoon.

Consider your target audience and timing modifications that align with their needs. Do you sell to tax accountants? They certainly have a busy time of year. Is it best to sell leading up to that busy time or immediately after that time? When does your customer typically have money to spend? How far before their budgeting cycle do you need to get their attention to get your product into the budget?

I was lucky enough in one of my early marketing jobs to work with a company that had been in business for a few decades. They were in a mature market with defined cycles. We didn't need to spend a lot of time iterating before we honed our timing to make the most of our campaigns. In some industries, especially new industries or industries in flux, finding the sweet spot in the timing of your digital marketing may take some trial and error.

Channel iteration

In Newfoundland, fisherman catch squid to use as bait to catch cod and other types of fish. So, one of the jobs in the fishing industry was to go out in the bay and catch squid. These fishermen were known as squid jiggers. Besides being a part of local lore and having a common meal named after them, Jigs Dinner, they had a saying that seems to be common wisdom in all the fishing ports, "Stay where you're at 'til they come where you're to." It seems the squid move around the bay and chasing them around is less productive than waiting for them in a place they will eventually come to.

I tell that story to lead up to this bit of wisdom: People aren't squid! Market interests move around, but sticking to one channel in hopes that your target market will eventually find you leads to running out of money before your best customer learns about you. A different strategy must be employed. You need to test the waters in multiple channels, then iterate to hone the mix of channels that leads to a positive ROI in each channel that you stay in.

In this case, look to a strategy employed by fly fisherman. On rivers, the fish tend to hold to one position and wait for food to flow to them. To catch them, you need to cast into a narrow zone upstream of them and let the fly drift into their feeding zone. The trick is to figure out where they're feeding, especially in cloudy water. The tactic here is to cast to structure, looking for "seams" in the current where fish expect to find food. You might cast a few times to one spot, then move onto another, looking for a response. When you do find a structure where fish are feeding, you can continue to pull fish from that and similar structures. On one little stream in Utah's Uinta Mountains, I found such a seam and pulled five fish out of the exact some spot. Since I was practicing catch and release, I don't know if I caught five fish or the same fish five times.

Digital "seams" have two distinct qualities. First, they are near structures where activity is taking place. This could be a busy social channel or streaming service where people – hopefully your target market – are feeding on content. Second, they are easily and cheaply accessible. You can push your content into the channel at a sustainable rate, allowing you space to test and iterate to find the right mix of timing, message, and frequency.

Response iteration

The great thing about digital marketing, verses something like direct mail, is the immediacy of the response. You can judge a campaign's success pretty quickly. This also gives you the opportunity to update your response mechanisms quickly. For instance, if you use landing pages as clickthrough endpoints from your campaign, you can see your clickthrough rate. If you present users with forms, you can see your form fill rate. If your forms are properly constructed, you can see when forms are abandoned, often at the exact field the respondent stopped entering information. This gives you, as a digital marketer, a huge advantage when it comes to iterating response forms.

Consider an example where you may have been the customer. Have you ever spoken to customer service for your phone service or to a bank and have them ask you to hold to complete a survey about how they did? Would it surprise you to know that the drop-off rate at this point in the interaction is upwards of 90%? What do you think the drop off rate is when people are asked to stay on the line for a "special offer to valued customers"? A lot more people stay on the line.

I talked about forms earlier. You need them to get information to figure out if someone is a qualified lead, but people value their time and privacy. You have to iterate your way to exactly what works best. Some people will drop off when you ask their name, other people will tell you anything you ask as long as you put that little "required" asterisk next to it. Most people are somewhere in between.

Keep in mind that a lot of information can be gathered in an automated way. You have to judge how you want to use that information. Maybe someone clicked through from an e-mail. Because you sent the e-mail, you likely know the name and email address of the person who clicked through. Do you still need to have them fill out a form? What does etiquette suggest? When they fill out the form they are giving you explicit permission to contact them directly. This raises the level of the relationship and increases the likelihood they will become a valuable lead.

Another aspect of form iteration may be the labels and text you put on the form. How inviting is your form? Are you making it clear to the customer how you intend to use their information? Are you explaining what's in it for them? Are you putting this context in a big block of text that's difficult to read or are you spoon-feeding the customer reasons to fill out the form field by field?

Iterating to better

You've likely heard the phrase "Perfect is the enemy of good." This is as applicable to marketing as any other field. We need to strive for good in our marketing, because perfect may never get launched, and an unlaunched campaign gathers no leads. Likewise, in our iterations, we shouldn't strive for perfect, but for better. By the time you get to perfect – which is a very expensive place to get to – conditions in the market change, and you're iterating again. Strive to be better, and sometimes you might happily land on perfect.

Attract

Two big benefits of iterating your outreach to prospects are, first, people want to see new stuff, and second, stuff can always get better.

If your material is funny, it's only funny the first few times. Follow up on the style with some fresh material, and it will continue to be funny. In fact, fresh material in the same style can often get a better humor response, because from the start of the piece, people are queued to be entertained.

Variations on a theme garner renewed attention and reinforce the memory of previous content. We see this most often in broadcast advertising – such as the GEICO ads mentioned above – but it should also be the case in blog articles, social billboards, short videos, and so on.

Iterate with multiple versions

Attraction content is usually short, which lends itself to creating variations. When you're trying to improve on your results, build a structured approach to your iterations. This may be a little bit of review and iteration working together. The simplest method is A/B testing. This method is easy to get your brain around and easy to explain results. As mentioned earlier, other, more complex methods exist or are waiting to be invented. The key to successfully monetizing your iterations is data. Gather it, review it, and iterate again.

A caution

Sharp departures from current marketing are expensive to get running and should be based on a shift in the market. "The creative team is bored" is not a compelling reason to make a hard change of direction.

Convert

In the conversion phase, you're often dealing with leads who are on the cusp of becoming customers. Other people in the company or in sales channels are going to be looking closely at the digital campaigns and collateral focused on converting leads. Iteration in the conversion phase often involves sales input as qualitative reporting from salespeople who have interacted with customers. If you are in a wholesale business, this feedback may be coming from retailers you sell to. Use caution with qualitative information. It's easy to get emotionally charged input from people at this phase that does not rely on data. Listen to their anecdotes or personal preferences, then either ask for data or offer to look into the data. Their anecdote about their one big client may be an outlier that if taken as the norm could derail a successful campaign.

Gaps and redundancies

When you think of conversion as a progression, iteration may not be so much about changing content as filling in gaps or removing redundancies. This often begins by asking questions and then constructing systems to answer those questions. Where did we ask the lead to take too big of a leap? Where did we bog down the customer's progression with too much overlapping or repetitive information? Where did our enthusiasm for content end up pushing messaging that cannibalized messaging that had yet to run its course? This last point often happens with the overuse of blogs, pod casts, and other serial content. You need to give serial content time to be read or viewed before you pile more content on top of it.

Retain

Within your own customer base, you should be able to iterate campaigns and content with pinpoint precision. You can use feedback data, customer survey data, frontline employee survey data, consumption data, and upsell data to iterate. Customers hopefully stay with you a long time, so – like in the attraction stage – consider iterating for freshness.

Summary

Every iteration needs to come with a cost-benefit analysis.

Consider your target audience and timing modifications that align with their needs.

Sticking to one channel or strategy in hopes that your target market will eventually find you leads to running out of money before your best customer learns about you. Test the waters in multiple channels, then iterate to hone the mix of channels that leads to a positive ROI in each channel that you stay in.

Use the immediacy of digital marketing feedback to amend forms and other feedback structures to improve data collection and customer progression between marketing stages.

Make sure campaigns are good, not perfect, because perfect may never get launched.

In your attraction marketing, iterate with multiple versions. Unless driven by clear data to move in a specific new direction, avoid making sharp departures in your attraction campaigns.

During the conversion stage, iteration in marketing focuses mainly on closing gaps and eliminating wasteful redundancies.

In retention marketing, you can pinpoint issues for iteration by using feedback data, customer survey data, frontline employee survey data, consumption data, and upsell data.

CHAPTER EIGHT

Curation

As your company rolls along, your marketing people will create new collateral and new landing pages for new products and campaigns.

Here's a fun email:

> "Please review the attached list of 4,100 pieces of marketing collateral and 2,750 web pages to determine what should be migrated to our new system. Please complete review by Friday."

This is the point in a company when you wish someone had set aside time to curate the content in your digital marketing system.

> **Curate** (*verb*): to select (the best or most appropriate) especially for presentation, distribution, or publication

Every piece of content that is current and useful should be added to your active content repository. Consider the following questions for each piece of content:

- What unique call to action does this content make in progressing the prospect, lead, or customer?
- Why was this content created?

- How is it or has it been used in campaigns?
- Are we likely to continue using this content in the near future?
- Is this content accelerating or decelerating our marketing efforts?
- Would we miss this content if we warehoused it?
- Does this content represent our current messaging and brand?

If your answers to these questions build a case for keeping the content, add it or leave it in your repository of accessible content. These are the pieces that are actively attracting prospects, converting leads, and retaining customers.

Everything else gets warehoused. If you think an out-of-date item could have value in future campaigns, maybe after it's rested for two or three seasons list it as such. For content that won't be reused, like campaigns in response to COVID, you should have a separate repository. Most organizations can get away with doing this once a year. For prolific marketing teams, who produce a lot of content and landing pages, this may be a semi-annual or quarterly process.

Deciding as a group

Do you like working in committees? Because this is one of those times when input from various stakeholders is essential. As the digital marketer, you can lead out and take the reins in gathering people to decide what to keep live, what to hold for later, and what to archive.

As noted above, the act of curation is deciding what to keep. I like to help the committee get started by considering a calendar, usually an annual calendar, of campaigns and initiatives. After reviewing what will be required for the calendar, you can mark old campaign and initiative items to go out of circulation. Next comes your on-going content. You should have data on these elements based on your review cycle. Data will tell you what's performing well and what wouldn't be missed if you archived it. This is also where people on the committee can express reasons to keep content that may seem low performing from a data standpoint but have a good qualitative reason for staying.

I remember coming across a customer case study about a large sports organization. The case study had very few views, even though it had been included in campaigns. The product marketing manager for the category pointed out that we were likely to have very few customers in this category, but when we did have one, it would be a big contract. Keeping the case study made sense based on a qualitative reason that it was the only case study in a category we were trying to grow. On data alone, you might miss opportunities that the larger team can see.

Warehouse vs. throw away

I mention creating repositories rather than throwing things away, for good reason. Out of the blue one day, while working at a software company, I got a call from the company legal office asking when we first used a catch phrase in our marketing. I tracked it down to a couple pieces of collateral created nine years earlier – pieces long out of circulation. My contact in the legal office was very excited and asked for the files, which I sent over. I wasn't privy to all the details or what legal was working on, but it seems that keeping stuff where you can find it can be important.

Finding that piece of old content was only possible because of good archive directory structures. Creating one folder for old stuff may not be your best option. Well-named files help you search for content, and creating good directories by content type, category, and the like will help you navigate directly to the things you need.

Finding curated content

A large warehouse store along Interstate 15 in northern Utah displays a billboard that says, "Everything you need, if we can find it."

Curated content is only as useful as your ability to find it. This requires some strategies and maybe even some technology as to how to make your content searchable. A robust taxonomy and the ability to create meta-data around your curated content can greatly aid your efforts. You can create dimensional tags such as industry, content type, product area, campaign, marketing phase, and so on to group your content and make it more searchable. Ownership is also a big part of determining the value of your content. Each piece should have an owner who can help answer the questions listed above.

Knowing where else copies of content may be stored is also crucial to curation. If you are pulling a video from your marketing system and repository, but a copy is posted on an external streaming service, you need to know that so you can pull that down as well. Too often, these kinds of things are only tribal knowledge in an organization and when people leave they get forgotten. Document all the places copies of files reside, so they don't pop up at the wrong time and place.

Competitive research

Let's say you've done some great competitive research that you want to share with your sales team. Take great caution in where you place this to share – unless you like fire drills. I've seen companies accidentally slide this content into their public facing repositories. It often started by being curated for the sales team and then lack of controls allowed it to be moved online by automated processes.

Attract

Curation of attraction content may call for a different storage mechanism than those at the later stages. This is because not every type of content in your attraction marketing resides in a stand-alone form. Take inline text messages for instance. In many companies, these are kept in spreadsheets or some other form of listable content – a database perhaps. Emails are also not something you would put on display for perusal by larger audiences inside or outside the company. Collections of banners in all their various sizes and shapes don't make for good standalone content either.

When you get to video ads and short video, you have reached content that makes sense to include in some sort of sharable way. If your content is share worthy, people will look it up and pass it along.

"Not yet" content

This may seem obvious, but you need a way to keep content within the bounds of the marketing group until it's time to be released. New content that's being prepared for an upcoming campaign needs to be shared with those working on the campaign but putting it somewhere that anyone can get it may allow it to be seen before it's ready. This may be something as simple as a funny banner ad being sent to a client before the release of the product it's touting. Content may contain links to webpages that have yet to be posted. Really troublesome content is anything that relates to price changes that aren't a part of company operations yet. When you tell customers that every plan in your cell service is now only $15 a month, your billing team had better be ready for that reality. Know the timing constraints on your material and treat access with care.

Convert

As you consider curating content designed to convert leads, progressive steps become very important. As discussed earlier, progressive steps are based on each piece's call to action. What are the invitations built into each piece, and how do they move the lead to the next step and eventually to purchase? Where in your curated content do you have gaps and redundancies? As you look at the concept of next steps in the conversion phase, you may begin to see that simply putting your content in alphabetical order in a repository is insufficient. Each piece of conversion content has a relationship to something before and after it.

I've occasionally written series of articles on a topic. These get posted over a series of weeks or months on a company or industry blog. Within each article, I reference the previous article and preview the next article. Depending on the control my client or I have over the blog, I may edit previous articles to put links into the most current article. This creates a chain of steps to move the reader along toward a full understanding of the topic and preparation for making a buying decision. Consider how you can best organize your curated conversion content to continue to fulfill its role in the progression toward purchase.

Retention

Retention content may be publicly available or retained in a customer-only space. This often depends on the amount of crossover the content has with content used in converting leads.

One of the biggest marketing purposes for curated content for customers is to introduce new customers to addons that aren't part of any currently running campaigns. Perhaps you created some addons to the product and made a big splash with customers at the time. Customers who have come on since then would not have been part of that upsell. They were likely introduced to the addons during onboarding but may not have been ready for them. Keeping your best customer content around ensures that customers still have access to it when they are ready to upgrade.

Marketing vs. support

As you curate content for retention, you may find it easy to conflate marketing content with support content. As someone who has written both marketing and support content, I can tell you that they are clearly not the same. Support content is often agnostic about whether you use a certain feature of the product. It simply tells you how it works and leaves the reasons to use it or not to use it up to you. Marketing on the other hand is about framing a call to action that will invite you to use the feature or upgrade the product. Good marketing content can sometimes sound like support, except for the fact that it is influencing a decision.

Summary

Develop a series of standard questions to ensure that every piece of current and useful content is added to your active content repository.

Input from various stakeholders is essential.

Keeping stuff where you can find it, even out-of-date stuff you won't use again can be important.

Curated content is only as useful as your ability to find it.

Curation of attraction content may call for a different storage mechanism than that for later stages. Keep content within the bounds of the marketing group until its time for release.

Curate conversion stage content according to progressive steps. These are usually identified by progressing calls to action.

Determine whether to curate retention stage content as publicly available or retained in a customer-only space.

References

Farris, Paul W.; Bendle, Neil T.; Pfeifer, Phillip E.; Reibstein, David J.; *Marketing Metrics*; Wharton School Publishing, 2006.

Fountain, Henry; "Hiking Around in Circles? Probably, Study Says"; *New York Times*; Aug. 20, 2009.

Moore, Geoffrey A.; *Crossing the Chasm*; Harper Business; 1991.

Moore, Geoffrey A.; *Inside the Tornado*; Harper Business; 2005.

"The marshmallow test: Bunkum or a true predictor of future success?"; https://bigthink.com/the-learning-curve/marshmallow-test/ ; Nov. 24, 2021.

Zaltman, Gerald; *How Customers Think*; HBS Press; 2003.

About the Author

Bob Shawgo started writing marketing copy in college more than 30 years ago and went on to lead successful marketing efforts in publishing, software, wholesale, education technology, media, business services, and bio-tech. As a consultant and employee, he's applied his marketing skills and mentored talented marketers in companies from start-ups to international brands. He currently runs Shawgo Group, a consulting firm, and writes articles and guides to help marketers and business builders find greater success in their marketing.

Made in the USA
Columbia, SC
02 May 2025